Time & Tide

Time & Tide

The History of the Harwich Haven Authority

1863 – 2013

By Graham Stewart

First published in 2013 by Wild ReSearch,
40 Great Smith Street, London SW1P 3BU

www.wildsearch.org

Harwich Haven Authority
Harbour House, The Quay, Harwich
Essex CO12 3HH

www.hha.co.uk

ISBN 978-0-9576966-0-0

Cover image: Harwich in 1750
© US Naval Historical Centre

Designed & typeset by
J. Schwartz & Co.

Printed in Great Britain by
Butler Tanner & Dennis Ltd

£15

To all who have kept the Harwich haven open and safe.

Contents

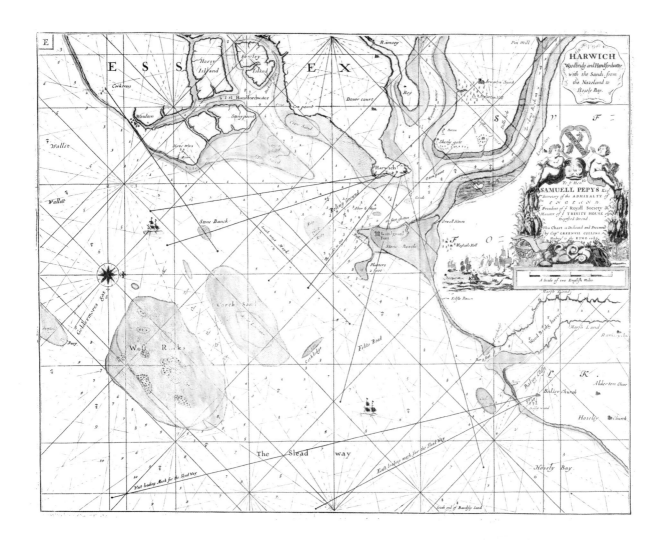

FIG I
Chart presented by
Captain Greenvil Collins,
Hydrographer to the
King, to Samuel Pepys,
1696

Foreword by the Earl of Cranbrook
(HHA Board member, 1989−97, vice-chairman 1995−97)

Glemham House has been occupied by my family for a century, and the library contains books of all sorts reflecting the varied interests of successive generations. Among these volumes, dating from the years when my father owned a Bermuda-rigged sloop, Arawatta, is the North Sea Pilot, part III, East Coast of England (ninth edition 1922) which, on p. 245, details: "HARWICH HARBOUR, entered between Landguard point and Beacon cliff a mile apart, is the only land-locked harbour between the Humber and the Thames, which affords complete shelter from all winds: though somewhat difficult of access, and though vessels of deep draught are restricted as to time of entry by tidal considerations, it is, nevertheless, of great strategical and commercial importance." Opening to the North Sea route from Scandinavia, and the nearest landfall on a natural route from continental Saxon, Frankish and, later, Hanoverian lands, the Haven has served as a focus for maritime trade and traffic and, in times of conflict, both a safe retreat and the mustering ground for our nation's naval forces.

Graham Stewart's absorbing history shows how these multiple values, ultimately derived from the topography of the Haven and the complexity of its sheltering offshore banks and shoals, has served sea-goers through the centuries from Roman times onwards.

The enduring value of this resource, however, has depended on constant attention and deliberate, planned intervention by those responsible for its vital functions. The combined estuary of the Stour and Gipping is naturally self-scouring on the ebb tide, but the strong coastal flow of North Sea currents and periodic violent storms imperil the integrity of the harbour and its approaches. King Henry VIII appointed Commissioners to examine the Essex shore and to safeguard its defences. Later, during the eighteenth and early nineteenth centuries, erosion on the Essex bank reached alarming proportions while, from the Suffolk shore, coastal drift and uncontrolled extraction of stone led to a huge extension of Landguard Point as a sand and shingle spit that threatened to close the harbour entrance. In 1844 the problems came to the attention of the House of Commons, which appointed Select Committees to examine the issues, and again in 1862. The second set of recommendations led to the passage of the Harwich Harbour Act, 1863, celebrated in this sesquicentennial year as the founding legislative measure for the present Harwich Haven Authority.

Graham Stewart tells how the 1863 Act established a Harwich Harbour Conservancy Board of nine members, four of whom were appointed by the Government. The Board was charged with the improvement of navigation in the estuary and given powers to fund its activities by a levy on larger users (initially 1d per ton on vessels exceeding 30 tons). In the 1870s, the Great Eastern Railway extended to Harwich and undertook the dredging needed to construct Parkeston Quay to provide a connection for Continental ferries. A counterpart connection was made on the north shore, with the formation of the Felixstowe Railway and Pier Company in 1875. In the expanding economy of the early twentieth century, increasing traffic and larger vessels required further dredging, aimed at providing a minimum depth of 20 feet at low tide. World War I saw a large involvement with the Armed Services and, when peace resumed, continued civil and military expansion. During World War II, Felixstowe's long pier was partly demolished, and in 1947 the port was considered too inconsequent to fall within the ambit of the National Dock Labour Scheme. Famously, Gordon Parker recognised the opportunities provided by freedom from the restrictive practices embedded in this Scheme — and so began the huge expansion of Felixstowe and Trinity Terminal, ultimately Britain's largest container port.

Through these years, the 1863 Act had been subject to a succession of amending Acts and Orders. These were consolidated in the Harwich Harbour Act 1974 which, among other things, defined both the bounds of the harbour and the limits of the Harwich seaward area, i.e., within a radius of four statute miles from the tip of Landguard Point as it had been in 1863. This Act was in force when, in October 1988, I was invited by the junior Minister, Lord Brabazon of Tara, to fill a forthcoming vacancy on the Board as the one person appointed by the Secretary of State for Transport to have "knowledge and experience of environmental matters affecting the area of the harbour". Official notification was received by the Board in December, and on 1st January 1989 I took up my appointment. Apart from s. 25 of the 1974 Act, giving the power to prevent pollution, there seemed to be no formal definition of my role. Through the Chief Executive, Victor Sutton, I sought advice on the Board's environmental responsibilities. The lawyers' reply recognised that no constitutional duties were specified, but itemised the principal Acts of concern (at that time): the Countryside Act 1968, Wildlife and Countryside Act 1981 as amended, Food and Environment Protection Act 1985, Control of Pollution Act 1974 and the Prevention of Oil Pollution Acts.

My appointment followed shortly after the final passage of the controversial Felixstowe Dock and Railway Bill 1988, which permitted the expansion of the Trinity Terminal beyond its previously agreed limits. A significant requirement placed on the developers was the provision of compensatory land and funding for the benefit of wildlife in the form of an 84-hectare landscaped nature reserve on Trimley marshes. Managed by Suffolk Wildlife Trust, this enterprise involved the creation of mixed habitats of nature conservation value — a freshwater lake, three lagoons, meadows and reedbeds, with public access. Retrospectively, this has produced a valuable new wildlife site within the estuary. At the same time, the Haven Authority (as it had become) undertook a huge dredging operation that deepened the navigation channel to meet the needs of ever larger container vessels. Environmental assessments had to evaluate not only the effects of the deepened channel on coastal currents and erosion patterns, but also the choice of disposal sites, the needs of the local fishing community and impacts on marine wildlife. HHA also bears responsibility for the buoys and lights that mark the navigable channel. On a couple of holiday trips by ferry to the Netherlands, I felt some reflected pride in checking and counting these vital aids to mariners.

As Graham Stewart has recorded, these years coincided with a decade of large financial transactions, from 1987 when P&O bought the port, through to 1998 when the major player, Hutchison Ports, acquired Harwich International, thereby uniting the main docks on the Essex and Suffolk banks of the Haven under single ownership for the first time in history. Although, as owners of Felixstowe, the exercise of pilotage was among the powers of Hutchison Ports UK, through skilful management and careful cost control HHA retained this vital service unchallenged. The design and commissioning of new pilot launches, using novel hull materials, was a significant item in Board discussions. Although not strictly within my terms of reference, I wanted to experience the full range of the Authority's activities. It was a great adventure to ride with the pilots — through a choppy sea

towards a "controlled collision" at the foot of the towering cliff of some vast container at the outer entrance of the dredged channel, or high on the bridge of a grain carrier out of Ipswich, steady down the Orwell between ranks of moored yachts. Thousands of yachts use the waters of the Haven and its approaches, and the safety of their sailors were, and still are a priority for HHA. For many years, an annual yachting guide and tidal forecasts have been published as a service to the yachting community.

In some aspects of environmental protection, the Authority could not act alone. The management of risk in the event of oil pollution incidents required cooperation of multiple bodies. The Haven Oil Working Group was set up and, in 1995, a protocol that committed resources for the control and clearance of an oil spill event was agreed between HHA, the National Rivers Authority, Ipswich Port Authority, Felixstowe Dock and Railway Company and Harwich Dock Company.

From the start of my appointment, my understanding grew of the role of part-time, non-executive member of the HHA Board with special responsibility for environmental matters. A fine example of leadership was provided by the chairman, Sir Colin Walker, and I was impressed by the competence in their respective fields shown by the Harbour Master and Director of Pilotage. My most direct interaction was with the Harbour Engineer, the late Richard (Dick) Allen, whose skills, acumen and sensitivity to the potential environmental impacts of his work were wholly reassuring. In my monitoring role, I learnt much about the intricacies of dredging, and environmental constraints and consequences. I record my respect for the senior officers of the HHA during my three terms as a Board member. It is pleasant that Graham Stewart's 150-year history of the Haven conservancy also concludes with brief biographical details of the present incumbents. I applaud the skills and dedication of the present crew on the bridge.

My father's yacht *Arawatta* was laid up in a creek at Iken during the war, and became mud-filled and derelict. But she was built of good Burmese teak, he found a buyer and I believe she sailed again. This might be an encapsulation of Graham Stewart's story of the rescue of a vital national resource from near disaster 150 years ago. I congratulate the author and all others involved in this timely, informative and forward-looking account of events leading to the present high status of the Authority as the leading example of a small handful of independent, non-commercial conservancies. Read on !

CRANBROOK, June 2013
Glemham House, Great Glemham

Acknowledgements

The publication of this book marks the 150th anniversary of the Harwich Haven Authority. It has been a privilege and pleasure to tap into the deep love for Harwich and its history from some of those who know it best — David Male, Bernie Sadler and the late Les Double. We would like to thank too the Harwich Society and Hutchison Ports (UK) Ltd for their assistance. To those and everyone else who has been so kind with their time and insights, the author is very grateful.

About the Author

Graham Stewart was educated at St Andrews and Cambridge universities. In addition to being the official historian of *The Times* newspaper, he has written histories across a range of economic, cultural, social and political themes, including *Bang! A History of Britain in the 1980s* and *Britannia: 100 Documents That Shaped a Nation* and the internationally acclaimed *Burying Caesar,* a study of the complex relationship between Winston Churchill and Neville Chamberlain.

Part One

"But Orwell coming in from Ipswich thinks that she

Should stand for it with Stour and lastly they agree

That since the Britans hence their first discoveries made

And that into the East they first were taught to trade

Besides of all the Roads and Havens of the East

This Harbour where they meet is reckoned for the best."

From the *Poly-Olbion*, a topographical survey of England and Wales put into verse
by Michael Drayton in 1612

Haven

"Haven" is a reassuring word. Since the early part of the Middle Ages it has come to mean a place of refuge. A "safe haven" is thus simultaneously a time-honoured figure of speech and a tautology. But its origins are strictly sea-faring. The Anglo-Saxons called the sea the *hæf*. Their word for a port was *hæfen*, similar to the Norse term for a harbour, *höfn*.

It was Germanic and Scandinavian mariners, sailing across the North Sea and navigating the treacherous sandbanks on the approach, who recognised the value of the natural *hæfen* or *höfn* in the estuary where the rivers Orwell and Stour meet. Nearly three miles wide and providing around 700 acres of good anchorage, this estuary offered perfect conditions for the mooring of longboats. Indeed, they had found the best natural haven on the east coast of England.

But they were not the first to scout the area, nor were they, at first, bid welcome. From the third century AD, Roman Britain had been constructing a line of fortresses and strong-points along what became known as the Saxon Shore in an effort to repel incursions by raiders. One such fort was built at Walton, near Felixstowe. Fragments of pavement tiled with geometric patterns, coins, and a ten to fifteen feet high rampart suggest a Roman camp once stood to the south of modern Harwich, while another rampart connected the camp to the summit of Beacon Hill. Other Roman artefacts have been unearthed west of Dovercourt.

An antiquarian writing his *Beauties of England* in 1776 claimed that a Roman wall had been pulled down within the last 20 years and that elephant teeth had been discovered nearby. Elephants in Essex? His conclusion was that they must have been the descendants of those that came over with the Emperor Claudius's invading army in 43 AD and were kept by the Romans as part of their military force.

With or without such beasts, the Romano-Britons manning the defence lines after the withdrawal of the Roman legions in 410 AD proved unable to hold out against the Germanic incomers who began making their way up the Orwell, Stour and other rivers and inlets of Essex and Suffolk. The most important were the Angles, who had sailed from the Baltic coast of what is now northern Germany and, from the sixth century, began establishing their kingdom of East Anglia. The Orwell-Stour haven was at the southern perimeter of this kingdom, marking the border with the smaller state established by the East Saxons (Essex).

By the beginning of the seventh century, it was East Anglia that had become the most important of the Anglo-Saxon kingdoms south of the Humber,

FIG 2
*The impression of a
seventh-century longboat
found at Sutton Hoo
in 1939*

FIG 3
*Silver Penny of King
Alfred the Great, c. 887*

its greatest king, Rædwald (reigned c. 559–c. 624), being considered a *Bretwalda* (Britain-ruler) and — while hedging his bets by retaining Pagan customs — a convert to Christianity.

Rædwald is commonly presumed to be the warrior-king buried with his ship and treasures at Sutton Hoo, by the banks of the river Deben near Woodbridge, east of Ipswich. When archaeologists excavated the burial mound in 1939 they discovered that although the oak ship had disintegrated, it had left an impression in the soil which gave a clear picture of its shape and dimensions. It was clinker-built with (surviving) iron planking rivets. It was 89 ft (27 metres) long, up to 14 ft (4.4 metres) wide in the middle and with a 4 ft 11 in (1.5 metres) inboard depth. There were oar-rests for forty oarsmen. While this was surely one of the finest examples of the longboats of the period, it gives a good indication of the design of those sea-crossing craft that would have moored in the Orwell and Stour.

During the ninth century it was Viking longboats that brought the next wave of invaders to the area. The haven was the perfect estuary for the Danes to use for resupplying their settlements and advances into eastern England. As the *Anglo-Saxon Chronicle* records, in what is the first surviving mention of the haven, it was in 885 AD that

sent King Alfred [the Great] a fleet from Kent into East Anglia. As soon as they came to Stourmouth, there met them sixteen ships of the pirates. And they fought with them, took all the ships, and slew the men. As they returned homeward with their booty, they met a large fleet of the pirates, and fought with them the same day; but the Danes had the victory.

The treaty that Alfred reaffirmed with the Viking warlord, Guthrum, in 890 conceded the loss of eastern England to Danish rule — the area known as the Danelaw. The Stour and Orwell haven was firmly within this territory and local place names attest to their origins as Danish settlements. However, the allegiance of those living there was far from being straight-forwardly Danish. In 917, East Anglia and Essex acknowledged the Saxon king of Wessex, Edward the Elder, as their overlord. In 991 and 993 Viking fleets sailed up the Orwell to plunder Ipswich. In 1016, Cnut (Canute) went ashore from the Orwell to claim the English crown, bringing the whole country, temporarily, under Scandinavian rule. By 1066, the land where Harwich now stands was owned by Ulwin, brother of King Harold. It would not be his for much longer.

Medieval Harwich

Despite all the evidence of nearby settlement by Romans, Angles, Saxons and Danes, Harwich still did not exist when Duke William of Normandy conquered England. If it had, then it would have been recorded in the Domesday Book.

What the great survey of land ownership carried out in 1086 did reveal was that King Harold's brother, Ulwin, was — like almost all the old Anglo-Saxon aristocracy — stripped of his possessions and that the new owner of the land on the south side of the Stour was a Norman supporter of William, called Aubrey de Vere, who later became Earl of Oxford.

While there was no mention of Harwich, the Domesday Book offers us a full audit of nearby Dovercourt

DRUVRECURT, which Ulwin held as a manor of 6 hides, is held by Aubrey in the demesne [property]. In the time of King Edward [the Confessor; i.e. in 1066] there were 8 villeins [peasants with tied obligations to the manor], now 6: there were then 6 bordars [young peasants], now 12. Then, as now, there are 6 serfs and 3 ploughs on the demesne and 6 ploughs belonging to the men. There are 3 acres of meadow with pasture for 200 sheep. There were then 3 rounceys [horses], 12 beasts, 200 sheep and 40 swine, and now the same. It was then worth £6 and now £12.

Besides what could be reared on land was what could be caught in the estuary. Tenant fishermen paid their dues to the manor for the right to fish from the banks, which they did by driving-in wooden poles into the water on the banks, upon which they constructed weirs with which to trap the fish. Whatever their effectiveness, these zig-zag constructions must have hindered the navigability of the river and were so well put-together than it was only with great effort that their remains were finally extracted from the riverbank in the nineteenth century.

It is not until the thirteenth century that Harwich — or Herewiz — first makes an appearance in surviving annals. By then, the Lord of the Manor of Harwich-cum-Dovercourt was the wealthy and influential Roger Bigod, Earl of Norfolk, and he took a decision which significantly bolstered the new town's prospects by granting it the right to operate a weekly market. This liberty greatly irritated the people of Ipswich who complained that the trade was bypassing them and going to Harwich. But the Earl of Norfolk was Earl Marshall of England and his will was not to be impugned. This, however, was but the first round in a centuries' long conflict between Harwich and Ipswich for the rights to trade supremacy and navigation levies upon the estuary.

War Port

Harwich's strategic significance was boosted by the onset of the Hundred Years' War, during which it became a port of assembly for the English navy. It was from the Orwell that King Edward III and Queen Philippa of Hainault sailed in 1338 with their invasion armada to France, via Antwerp. Eleven ships were left behind to guard the estuary from counter-attack. There was need for such precautions because the following year eleven French galleys sailed to the mouth of the estuary in a forlorn attempt to set Harwich on fire.

In June 1340, Edward III returned to Harwich in order to launch a yet greater fleet from the Orwell, and this armada of 200 ships was probably the largest single fleet ever to set sail from the haven. Off the coast of Flanders it met and engaged a French fleet of comparable size that was gathering with the intention of foiling the assault and then, in turn, invading England. The resulting battle of Sluys proved to be the greatest English naval victory up to that date. The French fleet lost around 160 ships, together with 16,000 men. Its hopes of repelling subsequent attacks, let alone invading England itself, were crushed and for the next 100 years the war would proceed to be fought out on French soil.

This was far from being Harwich's only role in the long conflict with France. For the siege of Calais in 1346, Harwich provided fourteen ships and

FIG 4
The Battle of Sluys

283 sailors — a considerable part of the town's adult manhood at that time in an action which secured the Channel port for England until 1558. With the Orwell acting as the frequent embarkation point for the English navy during the conflict, the war was certainly good for Harwich's development. In 1405,

it began building its own fort (on the north-east promontory of the town on the site subsequently occupied by the Naval Yard). A small harbour, the Town Quay, followed and this was connected directly to the castle. To the advantages of location provided by nature, medieval militarism was driving forward the infrastructure improvements that would make Harwich one of the great ports of England.

Yet, for all its defences, natural and manmade, Harwich remained far from invulnerable. By 1450, the war in France was effectively lost and the apprehension had switched to the likelihood of raids upon the English coast. In that year, the French finally managed a small act of retaliation with an audacious night-time raid on Harwich that resulted in nine deaths. In itself, the raid was little more than a smash-and-grab affair, and of little strategic significance. But shockingly, it was supposedly assisted by a local man, Adam Palmer, who as the Court Rolls puts it "showed to our French enemies the very secret way of our port of Orwell." We may deduce that the jury concluded that Palmer acted under duress because he survived the court's findings, being later listed as a crewmember of a Harwich ship.

For Harwich, the success of the raid necessitated a re-evaluation of its security and two years later the construction of superior defences was authorised and overseen by the Earl of Oxford. It was paid for by the free export of cloth from Ipswich by four Harwich merchants.

Render Unto Harwich … or Ipswich?

After 116 years, the war with France was concluded in 1453. Harwich's rivalry with Ipswich proved more protracted and, often, of more immediate concern to the inhabitants of both ports. In an age when closely guarded rights and charters prescribed which towns could engage in which activities, how frequently and at what levy, it was hardly surprising that Harwich, across from the mouth of the Orwell and Ipswich, the upstream but larger town, should vie for attention and supremacy.

The most intensely contested issue concerned which town enjoyed the right to levy dues from shipmasters using the haven. In 1380, King Richard II approved a petition from Ipswich guaranteeing that its inhabitants "have their haven to Polleshead granted to them, their heirs and successors." Polleshead — sometimes rendered Polles Hinnell — no longer exists, having been subsumed by the waves, though it was a promontory of land jutting into the sea beyond where Landguard Fort now stands. In effect, this gave Ipswich jurisdiction over all of the Orwell and the right to raise duties accordingly. These rights were affirmed and strengthened by King Henry VIII in 1513. To add insult to injury, the Ipswich bailiffs made clear that they interpreted their admiralty jurisdiction to include the eastern tip of the town of Harwich itself.

There were problems with this official favouritism towards Ipswich. With ships becoming bigger and Ipswich's approaches starting to silt-up (one particular problem was the habit of its townsfolk to dump their rubbish in the estuary, rather than have it carted away to London where it could be treated and recycled for new uses), Ipswich was becoming a less suitable port than Harwich. In 1565, the Commissioners admitted as much, writing that

the town of Harwich standeth at the mouth of the water that taketh his course to Ipswich and is of ancient time called Orwell haven which is of such depth before the said town of Harwich as any ship may come in and enter at a low water and diverse times the ships of foreign parts are driven to lie before the town for extremity of weather, sometimes of necessity of victuals and many times to make sale of such merchandise as they have in freight. And because there is neither Customer nor his deputy resident in the town, and their ships many times being of such burthen that they are not able to pass to Ipswich by decay of the Haven, and yet if they were they must observe the tides, which require sometime a longer abode than they are able to suffer, they are compelled to depart without making sale of their merchandise, to the great hindrance of the Queen's Majesty and her Custom.

Despite this, they concluded that "we think it not meet that the storehouse at Harwich should receive or discharge merchandise but such in cases of necessity" because Harwich's exposed position close to the sea made it an easier target for destruction by the French. Furthermore, were Harwich allowed to develop "it will be an utter decay to the town and port of Ipswich."

The haven's long-term development was ill-served by officialdom's efforts to prop-up Ipswich at the expense of Harwich. The expansion of the latter's harbour and boat-building capacity in the seventeenth century made the preservation of Ipswich's admiralty rights over the estuary look increasingly archaic. Eventually this reality achieved a nod of recognition. In 1693, Harwich gained admiralty rights over the river to Manningtree and towards Ipswich as far as Levington Creek. This did not end the disputes and mariners often found themselves having to pay dues to both jurisdictions. This unsatisfactory form of double-taxation continued formally until Ipswich lost some of her admiralty rights under the Municipal Corporation Act of 1835. To a lesser extent, there remained confusion until the formation of the Harwich Harbour Conservancy Board (as the Harwich Haven Authority was originally called) in 1863.

The Age of Discovery

By the sixteenth century, the broadening ambitions of Harwich's mariners were stretching far beyond the cod shoals off Reykjavik. Tales of the riches of Cathay, the spices and luxuries seeking merchants in China and south-east Asia, motivated the bravest. In 1553 Sir Hugh Willoughby set out from Harwich in his ill-fated attempt to discover the North-East Passage, the route from Europe to the Pacific through northern Russia's arctic waters. Unfortunately, Willoughby's ship got separated from that of the expedition's leader, Richard Chancellor. The following summer, the frozen bodies of Willoughby and his 62 crew were discovered by Russian fishermen off Lapland.

However, where Willoughby failed, Chancellor succeeded, dropping anchor at Archangel and meeting the Tsar, Ivan the Terrible, in Moscow. Tsar Ivan duly promised to open his northern domains to English traders. The result was the creation of the Muscovy Company whose royal charter of 1555 granted it a trading monopoly with Russia.

Not only was a scheme originally conceived to tap the wealth of the Far East diverted into trading with Russia; by being instituted as a joint-stock company, the Muscovy Company heralded a new form of capitalism. Instead of investors being sought to sponsor individual ventures for which they would receive a cut of any profits, they could buy and sell shares in an on-going company which could use the investment for multiple opportunities. This innovation was the principle behind what became the public limited company with shares tradable on a stock exchange. It was Harwich, along with London, that was the principal English port of this harbinger of modern capitalism, benefiting from a trade that saw English cloth being exported to Russia in return for Russian furs, timber (for taller sailing masts than domestic trees could provide), hemp, tar, wax and tallow.

Among the local mariners who pushed at the boundaries of the possible was Thomas Cavendish, who came from Trimley St Martin, on what is now the outskirts of Felixstowe. Between 1587 and 1588 he became the third person (after Ferdinand Magellan and Sir Francis Drake) to sail around the world. He did so in the *Desire*, a 120 ton, 18 cannon, Harwich ship. He was actually the first navigator to intentionally plan a circumnavigation. En route, he visited Africa, the Philippines, the coast of California, and picked up a couple of Japanese sailors who accompanied him the rest of the way. Already comfortably rich from an inheritance, the voyage brought him vast wealth, since en route he had plundered Spanish ports and shipping, including taking a 600 ton, Spanish galleon, the *Santa Anna* off Cabo San Lucas with

FIG 6
Thomas Cavendish,
'The Navigator'

its cargo of 122,000 silver dollars. This represented the single largest haul in history, at the time.

Still only 28 years old and already an MP, he was received by Queen Elizabeth I upon his return to England. However, the spirit that had driven his success also ensured his end. A subsequent voyage on the *Lester,* accompanied by John Davis and a 76-strong crew aboard the *Desire,* ended in tragedy with Cavendish's death near Ascension Island. The *Desire* battled on and discovered the Falkland Islands but all but 15 of the ship's complement died on board, before Davis was able to sail Harwich's battered little ship to Ireland in June 1593.

Along with Ipswich, Harwich dispatched three of its own merchant ships to help defeat the Spanish Armada in 1588 and these Harwich ships were probably among those that fought with the Spanish navy off Gravelines on 8 August. The flagships of the two main English commanders were mastered by Harwich men: Thomas Gray being master of Lord Howard of Effingham's flagship, the *Ark Royal,* while his brother, John Gray, was master of Drake's flagship, the *Revenge.*

Thomas Gray's daughter, Josian, married Christopher Jones, the master of the *Mayflower.* However, Harwich's associations with the New World pre-dated Jones's historic voyage. Thomas Cavendish had landed in Virginia in 1585 as part of a fruitless attempt to start a colony there. In 1607, another attempt was made, with an expedition sailing into Chesapeake Bay and establishing a settlement at Jamestown. This 100-strong expedition was led by another Harwich-born mariner, Christopher Newport, in his ship, the 120-ton *Susan Constant*.

Newport served on the colony's seven-man council, although with his return to London, conditions at Jamestown — which proved an ill-starred choice for a settlement — deteriorated. Despite three further voyages by Newport to resupply the colonists, they continued to succumb to disease, starvation and the mounting hostility of the Native Americans. He subsequently joined the East India Company and died in Java, in 1617, at the age of 57.

While Jamestown struggled on, it was the arrival of the Pilgrim Fathers in 1620 that shaped the defining self-perception of how America was colonised. The original 102 passengers (the majority of whom were economic rather than religious migrants, in addition to which there were around

FIG 7
*The English fleet harries
the Spanish Armada*

FIG 8
*Christopher Jones's house
on King's Head Street*

FIG 9
*A cutaway of the
Mayflower, showing
the interior layout for
its Atlantic crossing*

50 crew) huddled together on the near 3,000 mile journey to the New World in a Harwich ship, captained by a Harwich man.

The '*Mayflower* of Harwich' as the records originally described it, was built either in, or by, 1609. When not traversing the Channel with English woollens and French wines or going further afield (certainly to Norway and the Mediterranean, and perhaps as far as a whaling excursion off Greenland) she was probably moored at the end of King's Head Street — where her master and part-owner, Christopher Jones, lived (in a house that is still standing).

It is a matter of debate whether the *Mayflower*'s historic trans-Atlantic journey should be recorded as commencing from her home port of Harwich, either Wapping or Rotherhithe (where many of her passengers embarked), or Plymouth (where she docked awaiting an improvement in weather conditions and to take on passengers from the unseaworthy *Speedwell*). From there, the journey to Cape Cod took 66 days. Despite the loss of key members of his crew through disease, Jones was able to sail his *Mayflower* back to England in less than half the time, only 31 days. He reached Rotherhithe on 6 May 1621 where — after a subsequent trip to France — Jones was recorded as dying the following year.

Trading Haven

With weaving taking place throughout East Anglia at a time when the Low Countries were the centre of Medieval and Renaissance Europe's cloth trade, Harwich and Ipswich found themselves well situated ports to benefit from this commerce. Records for 1388 list some of the mariners and their goods that sailed in and out of the estuary, among them "the Cog *Anne* of Harwich leaves with cloth belonging to John Lucas of Manningtree … and John Bollard and his fellows have wheat in her" while "Cog *John* of Harwich leaves with cloth and wheat belonging to John Dawe and his fellows."

But wealth was built upon trading in other imports and exports as well and, as the names of those engaged in it suggest, Scandinavian merchants — perhaps members of the Baltic trading guild, the Hanseatic League — were among those sailing into the estuary: "Christian Arnaldson exports cloth, cheese and peas…. Arnaldesson imports ermine fells, madder and herrings. Wainscot and herrings enter in a Dansk vessel. Wheat, beans and peas are exported in the *Trynitie* of Harwich."

"In these coastes" wrote one report of the haven in 1588, "is very great traffique, but chiefly of English clothes, wooll, tinne, pewter, leade, saffron, sea coles, firewood and other commodities." A similar picture had been painted in another report three years earlier, albeit one populated by foreign traders and absent natives. According to the 1585 account, the sailors doing business in the haven were "all strangers and not one Englishman amongst them." Records for the Elizabethan and early Stuart period show butter, cheese and beer leaving the haven; the *Susan* importing bay salt from Rochelle and *Le Rasimus* and *Le Cristofer* taking billets and 20 barrels of "olei pranne" on from Harwich to London.

The reported prevalence of foreigners over domestic merchants was, in part, because so many of the town's own sailors were away fishing off Iceland between February and June. Complaint was made that there was scarcely 20 able-bodied men to defend the town from attack. Yet, for most of the pre-industrial centuries, fish was the single greatest mainstay of the haven's economic activity. What began as a heavily localised activity, with weirs to trap fishes along the estuary's banks spread, during the sixteenth century, to the deployment of Harwich's fishing fleet to as far as the waters off Iceland.

The changeable sea and weather were not the only hazards confronting the small boats in their search for cod. They also faced attack from Spanish ships and pirates or arrest for straying into the territorial waters of foreign powers. This fate befell the "good shippe, the *Barke Kinge* of Harwich," a 140 ton fishing boat that Danish customs officers seized. Its cargo was confiscated and its master, John Scrutton, detained in a Danish prison. Attack by French and American ships during the latter's War of Independence also proved to be an occupational hazard: on one day alone 25 of Harwich's fishing fleet were seized by the French navy — which would have been a calamitous turn of events but for Louis XVI's magnanimous granting of the men's freedom along with an instruction to his sailors to leave British fishermen alone. Unfortunately, such gentlemanly behaviour was less evident when war recommenced in 1793. For all the loud protestations about liberty, equality and fraternity, France's revolutionary regime was far less charitable in its dealings with Harwich's sea-fearing labourers.

What types of fish and what quantity changed over time. As a Church-prescribed meat on specified days, fish especially made up a significant part of the local diet before the Reformation. On the one hand this brought to the fishing fleet a secure market, on the other, it made it subject to price controls (the Church's thinking being that since everyone needed to eat fish, its price should be fixed at an accessible rate). Price-fixing was established by giving the churchwardens and chamberlains of the Guild of St George a monopoly on the distribution of herring. King Henry VII had to warn Harwich's townsfolk that if any of them bought herring from another source, they risked a 40 shilling fine "to the Lord." Another Tudor ruling established that

If anyone happens to buy any herrings within the town of Harwyche he shall allow his neighbours, inhabitants of Harwyche to have part thereof, paying equally and also paying to the Church of St Nicholas of Harwich a halfpenny per hundred according to the use and custom used time without mind on pain of forfeiting to the Lord £3 6 shillings and 8 pence whereof half to the Lord, the other half to the use of the church.

Regulations of this kind were undermined by the arrival of Protestantism and, thereafter, a less regulated approach to the market.

Harwich's fishing fleet appears to have gone into relative decline during the seventeenth century only to recover in the eighteenth. In 1720, the town was sending out 12 smacks, whereas by 1774 that number had increased to 62 and to 74 by 1792. Two reasons for this were the discovery of a new cod ground and the development of a co-operative system that allowed the cost of a new smack to be spread through a share scheme embracing all those engaged in its fitting and supplying it. About 500 men were being employed in Harwich's fishing industry by this time. As the *Harwich Guide* of 1808 boasted

This number of fishing smacks now, and for several years past … are equal, if not superior, to any number fitted out from or belonging to, all other ports in the kingdom … The port of Harwich has been for many years the principal fishing town near London and from whence the tables of our nobility and gentry are principally supplied with excellent live cod, haddock halibut, skate, coal-fish and whitings … Several fish machines run from Harwich in a very expeditious manner to supply the London market.

In the 1780s, the ever inquisitive traveller, François de Rochefoucauld, examined Harwich's 'cod smacks' and noted down his impression, "they are of a peculiar construction: very short, and the planking is twice as thick as that of an ordinary vessel and is lined with lead in order to hold water and bring in the cod alive. Each can cost up to a thousand pounds to build." His pricing was at the upper end of the market, around £650 being more typical. Another curious foreigner, Maximilien de Lazowski, added detail about how — in the pre-refrigeration age — the smacks could be out at sea for many days and yet still deliver their catch fresh

In the middle of the hold are two tanks … six or seven feet long … the bottom of the boats, under the tanks, is pierced with holes an inch in diameter to admit the sea-water in which the cod swim until they reach London. They reckon these sloops make as good speed as any other, despite the sieve-like effect of the holes.

From the 1830s onwards, Harwich's fishing industry commenced upon its long decline. No matter how "expeditious" were the Regency-era "fish machines" taking Harwich's catch to the tables of the nobility and gentry, such wagons were no match for steam locomotion. By the time the railway came to Harwich, in 1853, rival east coast ports, already connected, had stolen a march.

For much of the Victorian age this decline was gradual. Even in the 1890s, there were still 21 cod smacks setting out from Harwich, together with 37 smaller boats looking for whelks (which were used as bait on the five mile long lines dragging behind the cod smacks). Up to 300 fishermen were still engaged in the industry. Thereafter the decline gathered momentum. A sign of how under-capitalised Harwich's fishing industry had become is suggested by the fact that it was not until the Edwardian period that its fishing boats switched from sail to motor, with the last cod smack, the *Gypsy*, folding-up its sails for the final time in 1913.

By the eve of a second world war, Harwich's fishing industry was down to 17 active boats and 60 men.

Shipyard

During the seventeenth century, Harwich's importance grew as an east-coast port and a centre of shipbuilding. Nevertheless, it was greatly outstripped by London. With the development of the Port of London, the shipyards at Poplar and Deptford expanded to Harwich's detriment. But while private shipbuilding declined, the patronage of the state assumed far greater significance.

Until the seventeenth century, Harwich's role as a building and refitting yard for ships of — or used by — the Royal Navy had been sporadic. Periodically, the town's merchants would receive state bounties to commission ships "to the increase of our Navy of this Realm" which could be put at the monarch's disposal in time of war. These were built by private yards on the town's front near where the Halfpenny Pier now stands. A sense of the scale of the operation is provided by the register of shipping of 1582 which reveals that of the 177 vessels in England exceeding 100 tons, nine of them came from Harwich and eight from Ipswich.

Improvements to ship design brought larger vessels. While Harwich's largest ship in 1582 had been of 140 tons, during the reign of King James I this had increased to 240 tons. The decisive step in expanding Harwich as a shipbuilding port came during Cromwell's republic, when the government took out a 99 year lease at £5 a year from the town corporation in order to construct a permanent wharf and building yard. The result was the Naval Yard on the site of the old Town Quay.

Under the watchful eye of its commissioner, Nehemiah Bourne, the Harwich Naval Yard quickly gained a reputation for efficiency. As General Monck observed in 1653 to an Admiralty committee, "it is strange that twenty ships should be so long fitting at Chatham, Woolwich and Deptford, where there are so many docks … when there have been twenty-two or more fitted out from Harwich in half the time by Major Bourne." Possibly not unrelated to this impressive rate of productivity was the fact that Bourne's methods included suppressing Harwich's previously flourishing alehouses.

With the monarchy's restoration in 1660, Bourne emigrated to the American colonies, but the Harwich Naval Yard continued to prosper. Between 1660 and 1827, 56 men-of-war were built there. Among them was HMS *Harwich* (the second of six Royal Navy ships to bear this name), a 70 gun ship of the line, in 1674, and which Samuel Pepys considered among the finest in the navy.

The *Harwich* was built to the designs of Anthony Deane whose 1670 work, *Doctrine for Naval Architecture*, was considered among the greatest treatises on its subject. Responsible for

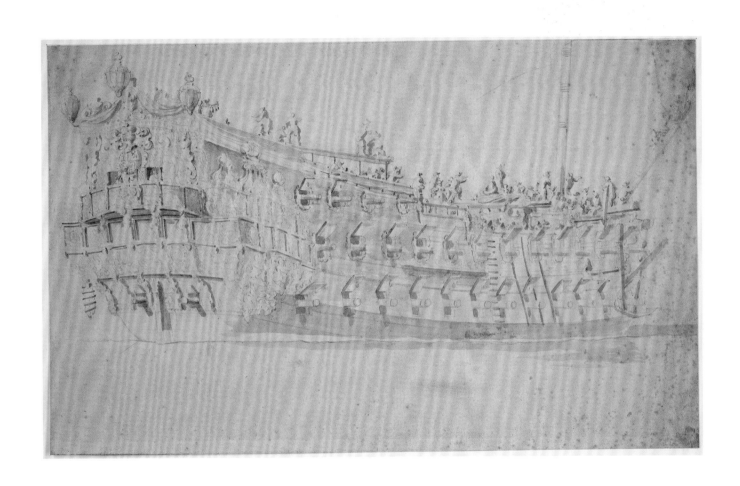

FIG 10
HMS *Harwich*

more than 20 warships, Deane's contribution to Harwich's renaissance as a Royal Navy shipyard was intimately entwined with the career of his friend and patron, Samuel Pepys. It was Pepys who, as Charles II's Clerk to the Acts of the Navy Board, secured for Deane the position of Master Shipwright at the Harwich Naval Yard and both men served simultaneously as MPs for Harwich (the town returned two members of parliament) first, briefly, in 1679 and then from 1685 until 1689. Deane also served as Harwich's mayor and funded the building of its jail and a new guildhall.

With a particular speciality in constructing small and medium-sized fighting ships, Harwich's Naval Yard was never the equal of those at Chatham or Portsmouth. But it did important re-fitting work and was especially busy repairing damaged warships during the Anglo-Dutch wars of the 1660s.

During the period of Deane and Pepys, the English Admiralty (Scotland retained its own navy – of four ships – until 1707) owned five naval yards: besides Harwich, there was Portsmouth, Chatham, Deptford and Woolwich. Harwich built 14 of the 80 warships constructed between 1660 and 1688.

In the 1780s, the travelling French aristocrat, François de la Rochefoucauld, was surprised to be allowed into the Naval Yard – Harwich's was the only one in Britain where such curiosity was permitted. "I walked in and saw two frigates building, to be named *Pollux* and *Hannibal*" he recorded, before adding, "Perhaps we shall capture them?" With the return to cross-Channel hostilities, his hopes were, briefly, realised. The 32-gun, *Pollux,*

FIG 12
Samuel Pepys

renamed *Castor*, was indeed captured by the French off Brest on 10 May 1794, only to be retaken nine days later. It ended its days as a floating prison off Portsmouth. *Hannibal*, admired by a French captain for its ability to "sail like a witch", fought the French off the West Indies before getting grounded and forced into surrender at Algeciras bay in 1801. In that same year, the 74-gun HMS *Conqueror* was launched from the Naval Yard and proceeded to fight with distinction at the Battle of Trafalgar.

The Admiralty Board had ceased to exercise direct control over the Naval Yard in 1713. However, Royal Naval ship-building continued on the site under private ownership until the launch of the 74 gun HMS *Scarborough* in 1812. The conclusion of the Napoleonic Wars three years later and the retrenchment that followed ensured no more commissions from the Admiralty. Ten steamers for commercial use were the last vessels to be built there. With their completion between 1825 and 1827, the Yard's ship-building days ended.

Protecting the Haven

In January 1588, six months before he was to command Queen Elizabeth I's fleet as it sailed out to engage the Spanish Armada, Lord Howard of Effingham paid a visit to Harwich. Many years had elapsed since his last visit there and coming to the haven with fresh eyes made him see clearly the value of what lay before him. To Lord Burghley, he wrote

> it is a place to make much of for the haven hath not its fellow in all respects not in this realm, and specially as long as we have such enemies so near us as be in the Low Countries, and not more assured than we are of Scotland. My Lord we can bring of all the ships that Her Majesty hath, around there in 3 springs. I know not that we can do so in any place else but here in Harwich.

For such an asset, the quality of its defences was lamentable. Only the remnants of the town's medieval fort still existed. In 1543, King Henry VIII had ordered the construction of a new fort to guard the estuary, but this proved to be a mean affair, consisting of two blockhouses surrounded by earthworks. Within nine years, it was already deemed to be in such poor repair that it was stripped of its principal armament when its cannons were taken back to the Tower of London.

FIG 13
Lord Howard of Effingham. As Queen Elizabeth I's Lord High Admiral, he was chief commander of English forces against the Spanish Armada

FIG 14
*The Dutch ship in the
centre of this painting
is de Ruyter's flagship,
Zeven Provincien, which
ran aground during his
attack on Harwich on
2 July 1667*

Thus the haven lay exposed until Landguard Fort was re-provisioned between 1626 and 1628 with an earthworks and wooden stockade. In 1666 this was strengthened with the construction of brick ramparts, an improvement that proved timely. The Second Anglo-Dutch War had broken out. In June 1667 the Dutch captured the fort at Sheerness, sailed up the Medway, caused grievous damage to the Royal Navy at its base in Chatham and blockaded the Thames estuary. Their next step was to seize the Harwich haven.

On 2 July, about 60 Dutch men-of-war appeared off Harwich. The plan of attack was masterminded by Admiral Michiel De Ruyter, with the landings led by Colonel Thomas Dolman, an Englishman who had fought with the Parliamentarians in the English Civil War and who, with the Restoration of the monarchy, had offered his services to the Dutch Republic instead.

De Ruyter intended his ships to pummel the garrison at Landguard Fort from the seaward side, while simultaneously using the rest of his squadron to sail into the estuary and land troops to attack the fort from the landward side. But Dutch reconnaissance on the depths of the estuary was inaccurate and finding the approaches dangerously shallow, the assault was called off after De Ruyter's flagship briefly ran aground. This left the bulk of the marines — about 1,500 in all, armed with "grenadoes" — to be landed at Cobbold's Point, from where, under cover of a dense smoke-screen, they advanced south to the Fort, dragging-up their cannon from the beach and bringing with them ladders and climbing apparatus to scale the Fort's 20 ft ramparts.

Supported by the local militia, the garrison was composed of the Duke of York and Albany's Maritime Regiment of Foot (a forerunner of the Royal Marines), under the command of Captain Nathaniel Darell. Combined, the defenders numbered under a thousand. Yet, while outnumbered by a ratio of 3:2, they had the artillery advantage of 40 cannon firing from the Fort. Despite repeated charges, the Dutch marines were cut down. The marksmanship of English musketry was supplemented by the firing of grapeshot which smashed into the shingle, turning it into lethal shrapnel. Driven back under this withering fire, the Dutch sustained around 150 casualties, including the death of their commander, Dolman, before managing to re-embark in the early morning light, the mission aborted.

The defenders had suffered scarce ten casualties. Excluding the farcical French landing of 1797 on the Welsh coast at Fishguard, the battle of Landguard Fort proved to be the last time a foreign invading force was repulsed on English soil.

No such hindsight was gifted to those entrusted with the defence of the realm at the time and while the threat from the Dutch Republic receded in the first half of the eighteenth century, that from France remained. In particular, there was the near-constant threat of a French-assisted invasion by Jacobites intent on overthrowing the Hanoverian monarchy and restoring the Catholic house of Stuart.

FIG 15
Landguard Fort from the air

FIG 16
*Harwich Redoubt,
guarding the approach
to the haven from
the Essex banks. The
cranes of Felixstowe
docks now rise from
the Suffolk bank*

Following the first Jacobite Rebellion, a new battery was added to Landguard Fort in 1717. Visiting it, the novelist and Government agent, Daniel Defoe, was impressed. He adjudged that it made the haven entrance "one of the best and securest in England," and marvelling at how

the making this place, which was formerly no other than a sand in the sea, solid enough for the foundation of so good a fortification, has not been done but by many years labour, often repairs, and an infinite expence of money, but 'tis now so firm, that nothing of storms and high tides, or such things, as make the sea dangerous to these kind of works, can affect it.

Defence technology, however, quickly moved on, and in 1744, on the eve of the second Jacobite Rebellion, a complete rebuilding of Landguard Fort commenced. Despite subsequent — mostly Victorian — remodelling which altered the layout and look of the fort, this created the pentagon-shaped structure with bastions at each corner that exists today.

As the imminent threat of attack returned with the Napoleonic Wars, so Landguard Fort was supplemented by other defence works. Of the 103 circular Martello Towers built along the English coast to house batteries against the expected attack, seven were built around what is now Felixstowe. Two became victims to erosion, one collapsing into the sea as early as the 1830s. A third, on Bath Hill, was assimilated into the building of the Bartlet

Hospital in 1926. Four remain, of which one used to be the Coastguard Station.

Of these Napoleonic War additions, the most important was the Harwich Redoubt, to the south-east of the town, built on the Essex approach to the estuary directly opposite Landguard Fort on the Suffolk side. Greater than the Martello towers, this imposing circular fort was armed with ten cannons and protected by a moat around it to deter commando raids (a single drawbridge provided access).

Thus it was only on the eve of Napoleon's defeat at 1815 that the haven was properly defended on both sides of the approach. Although the largest guns were eventually removed, and the Redoubt was abandoned in 1920, the haven remained guarded by a coastal battery until 1956, when the last of the garrison finally departed Landguard Fort, leaving it and the Harwich Redoubt to succumb to decades of neglect before English Heritage, the Landguard Fort Trust, and the Harwich Society began the task of preservation and restoration.

The Port for the Post

In 1661, Henry Bishop, the Postmaster General, reached agreement with Syman van Horne who was acting for the City of Amsterdam to commence a regular packet boat service to convey "Common Mayle." The service would run between Harwich and Hellevoetsluis, the Netherlands' principal naval base, on the Haringvliet, six miles south of the Maas estuary which led into Rotterdam.

Harwich had found itself informally used as a port in which merchants would bring with them letters and documentation. But until 1661, it was Folkestone that had been the officially contracted packet station between England and the Low Countries. The awarding of the service to Harwich was a major coup for the port. Coaches arrived there from London carrying the mail, which was then transferred onto sailing boats (sloops of 60 tons) for the approximately 110 nautical miles journey. Passengers could also pay to travel with the mail, many of them diplomats, merchants or bankers on their way to, or from, the great seventeenth century financial centre of Amsterdam. Indeed, bills of exchange and stock market information soon became a significant part of the mail.

Scarcely had the service begun than the outbreak of the Second Anglo-Dutch War caused its suspension. But with the signing of the Treaty of Breda in 1667 it was restored with a twice weekly service from Harwich departing on Wednesdays and Saturdays and sailing to Brill until concern at the hazardous nature of its shallow approaches ensured a return to Hellevoetsluis. Passengers were charged 12 shillings for the better berths, and half that for those travelling steerage class. No service to Antwerp was possible: since 1585 the Dutch had closed access to the Scheldt in their dispute with the Spanish occupiers of what is now Belgium. Apart from a brief period during and immediately after the Napoleonic wars, it remained closed until 1863.

If Harwich had a defect at this time it was not one of location but of the casual attitude of its townsfolk towards those who were brining money into the area. Writing in 1724, Daniel Defoe reported that

> Harwich is known for being the port where the packet-boats between England and Holland, go out and come in: The inhabitants are far from being fam'd for good usage to strangers, but on the contrary, are blamed for being extravagant in their reckonings, in the publick houses, which has not a little encourag'd the setting up of sloops, which they now call passage-boats, to Holland, to go directly from the river of Thames; this, tho' it may be something the

longer passage, yet as they are said to be more obliging to passengers, and more reasonable in the expence, and as some say also the vessels are better sea-boats, has been the reason why so many passengers do not go or come by the way of Harwich, as formerly were wont to do; insomuch, that the stage-coaches, between this place and London, which ordinarily went twice or three times a week, are now entirely laid down, and the passengers are left to hire coaches on purpose, take post-horses, or hire horses to Colchester, as they find most convenient.

During the seventeenth century, three sloop-rigged hoys undertook the service. By 1730, four boats were doing so: the *Prince*, the *Dolphin*, the *Eagle* and the appropriately named *Dispatch*, carrying between 100 and 150 passengers and crew combined. In 1786, the founder of Methodism, John Wesley, boarded one of their successors at Harwich, the *Bessborough*, which he declared "one of the cleanest ships I ever saw with one of the most obliging captains." The German novelist, Sophie von La Roche, found herself on the return journey with the 83-year-old Wesley, and recorded:

Two rooms and two cabins hold 26 berths for passengers; it is all very attractive. The outer room is panelled with mahogany and has a fine mirror and lamp brackets fastened to the wall. The berths are arranged along the side walls in two rows, like theatre boxes, one above the other; they have thoroughly good mattresses, white quilted covers, neat curtains, and on

a ledge in the corner is a chamber made of English china used in case of sickness. In order to lie down, the outer board of these boxes is removed and then fitted in again by the sailors to prevent people from tumbling out. It holds one person quite comfortably and the whole looks very neat.

No amount of plush fittings could prevent a rough crossing. Sophie von La Roche spent most of the 48 hour voyage feeling sick and confined to her bunk. Wesley left a colourful account of proceeding above and below deck

The rolling of the ship made us sick. I myself was sick a few minutes; Mr Broadbent, by times, for some hours; Mr Brackenbury (who did not expect to be at all) almost from the beginning of the journey to the end. When we had been twenty-four hours on board, we were scarce come a third of our way. I judged we should not get on unless I preached, which I therefore did, between two and three in the afternoon, on 'It is appointed unto men once to die'; and I believe all were affected for the present.

Affected or otherwise by these intimations of mortality, on that particular voyage there were 22 passengers and their identity gives an insight into the nature and business of those who used the service. Besides the Methodist preacher and his followers and the aristocratic female German novelist, there was Captain Webb, his wife and sister-in-law, Miss Lake and a cousin who had

been travelling through France, Flanders and to the health resort of Spa, an American captain who had recently fought under General Nathanael Greene in the War of Independence (which had ended only three years previously),"an Englishman from Falkland Isles" (a very early settler indeed, since the British presence there only dated from 1766) and another Englishman who had spent time in Patagonia, a Mr de Moulin from the Hague and his "charming daughter," a French language tutor based in Geneva, and "a wealthy young farmer" who had gone to Rotterdam to visit the *Kermesse* fair.

The relative stagnation of the Dutch economy in the eighteenth century did little to harm the packet trade since the Harwich-Hellevoetsluis route also served to carry the despatches between the courts of London and Hanover too. Besides kings (William of Orange, George I, George II) arriving at Harwich from the continent were future and past queens (Princess Charlotte of Mecklenburg-Srelitz on her way to marry George III; the weighty corpse of Queen Caroline on its way back to Brunswick), princes (Frederick, Prince of Wales), escaping foreign royalty (it was to Harwich that the remnants of the French royal family arrived to begin their English exile from their homeland), diplomats and spies. Also among those taking the Harwich packet was James Boswell, en route to study Law at Utrecht University in 1763. Dr Johnson followed him as far as Harwich where they dined together in one of the town's inns.

Different reports contest the prosperity that the packet trade brought to the haven in the eighteenth century. François de La Rochefoucauld was not greatly impressed, writing in 1784 that "the town

FIG 17
*Harwich in 1750.
Note Landguard Fort
on the Suffolk bank*

is badly built, the streets are narrow and without alignment, the gutters don't drain the water off the streets, it is full of mud, even in summer.… The port is nothing much." His attitude was not helped by "a very bad dinner in a very bad inn."

Half a century earlier, Defoe had given a more even-sided account, declaring in his *Tour Thro' The Whole Island of Great Britain* that "Harwich is a town of hurry and business, not much gaiety and pleasure; yet the inhabitants seem warm in their nests, and some of them are very wealthy." A few families, enjoying the official preferment that came with the Post Office's licensing the packet service, trimmed off a good living and, perhaps, turned an occasional blind eye to smuggling and other activities that escaped the attention of His Majesty's customs officers. When the *Bessborough* and the *Prince of Wales* were seized in 1774 and found to have contraband goods on board, their captains (who were also the boats' owners) had to pay fines, respectively, of £306 and £272 (reflecting the contraband's high value) half of which went to the Exchequer and half to the customs officer who made the search. These fines either failed to deter or may even have encouraged greater smuggling in order to make good the expense, for the two boats together with the *Dolphin* were caught for the same offence three years later. As Defoe put it, while there was clearly money being made in Harwich, "there are not many (if any) gentlemen or families of note, either in the town, or very near it."

During the successive wars of the eighteenth century, maintaining the packet service was potentially hazardous, forcing the boats to be armed with up to four cannon to repel attempts at seizure. In 1777 the Harwich packet boat, *Prince of Orange*, was captured by USS *Surprise*, a sloop in the service of the American revolutionaries. When Britain again went to war with France in 1793, it was the two other packet services (Falmouth to Corunna and the Dover cross-Channel route) that were closed, leaving Harwich as the only port to continue taking and receiving continental mail. The route to Hellevoetsluis was supplemented with new routes to Cuxhaven at the mouth of the Elbe, Husum in Schleswig-Holstein and Gothenburg in Sweden. In 1795, with the French invasion of the Low Countries and fall of the Dutch Republic,

the Harwich packets had to be stopped, a Yarmouth in Norfolk to Cuxhaven service keeping Britain's continental communications open.

The Harwich service recommenced in 1802 to Cuxhaven, Husum and Gothenburg and soon thereafter to Hellevoetsluis. With Harwich again the only operating packet port this was the period of its greatest importance, and the number of services were increased accordingly as news and diplomatic communications criss-crossed between Britain and the courts of its European allies in the ever shifting coalitions against Napoleon.

Only with Napoleon's defeat at Waterloo was Harwich's monopoly lost, the Dover services to Calais and Ostend restarting and soon proving the more significant routes, with far shorter sailing times (it was a quarter the distance between Dover and Calais as between Harwich and Hellevoetsluis), better road communications at either end and higher passenger revenues. During the 1820s, steamers — which had greater tonnage — started operating from Dover while Harwich persevered with sail-power alone. The Post Office's contract was awarded to the General Steam Navigation Company which, from 1834, left for the continent from the Thames estuary. The service to Gothenburg was awarded to Hull.

With these blows, Harwich's days as the centre of the packet service ended. It seemed its role as a port was imperilled too.

FIG 18
The Harwich Packet Boat,
Prince of Wales, is captured
by the USS Surprise during the
American War of Independence

Part Two

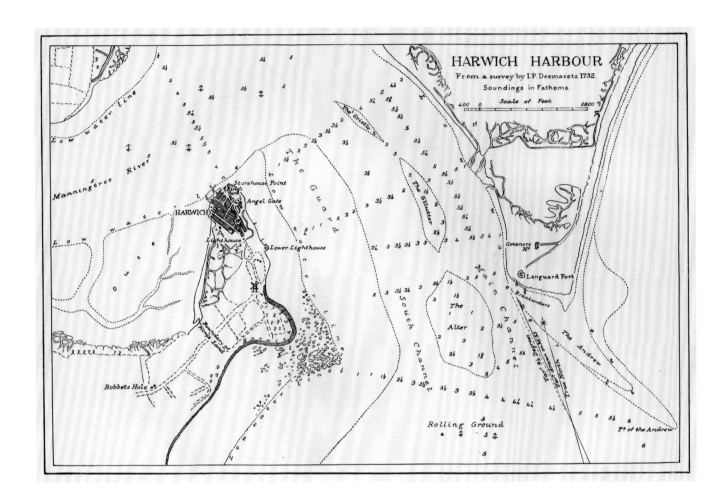

FIG 19

The survey of Harwich Harbour made in 1732 by the military engineer John Peter Desmaretz. A naturalised Briton, Desmaretz was a surveyor to the Board of Ordinance and a prolific harbour engineer

Time and Tide

Where the Orwell and Stour met, nature had created the ideal haven. But nature's work did not stop and nor did the human activities that affected it.

There appears to have been little serious dredging work undertaken during the Medieval centuries — the absence of which upstream in the Orwell helped seal Ipswich's fate as a major port. The Harwich townsfolk's vehement opposition to the removal of stone from the cliff to be taken away to build Cardinal Wolsey's (later aborted) college in Ipswich in 1528 demonstrated their awareness of how tampering with the coastline could affect the power and course of the estuary's tide. If their descendants, 300 years later, had possessed the same far-sightedness then much of the haven's mid-nineteenth century problems might have been averted.

Some erosion at the mouth of the haven was evident in the Tudor period nevertheless. A sixteenth-century map of the coast suggests that Harwich's harbour entrance was a little to the north-east from its current location. Tides shifted shingle southwards, narrowing the haven entrance and gradually shifting the harbour entrance south-westwards. Fortunately, the estuary's ebb tide prevented the entrance from silting up too swiftly and the depth does not seem to have changed much until the nineteenth century.

The greatest concern was from a swift collapse along part of the coastline. The constant battering it was taking from the sea risked a potentially devastating demolition in the natural defences that could cause Harwich itself to be engulfed by the waves. This was no idle speculation. Two great storms in 1286 and 1287 had swept much of the Suffolk port of Dunwich into the sea, a calamity that reduced what was one of medieval England's most thriving towns (with a population of at least 3,000) into the quiet village it has been ever since.

King Henry VIII visited Harwich in 1543 and assigned £400 for its "waterworks." It was during his reign that commissioners were first appointed to examine the coastline of Essex where "the walls, ditches, banks … and other defences by the coasts of the sea … by rage of the sea flowing and reflowing are much damaged … and it is to be feared that greater loss … be like to ensure unless speedy remedy be provided … The Commissioners or some of them shall always be there to survey the walls … and cause them to be repaired and also to enquire of honest and lawful men of the shire concerning defaults and avoidances."

The degradation of the harbour was again a concern in 1580, when £5 fines were introduced on any who threw ballast or rubbish into the harbour or took rock from Beacon Cliff. Bailiffs were empowered to take immediate steps to plug any breaches in the sea-walls.

A 1588 guide to the ports and rivers from London to Harwich provided mariners with navigation advice on how to enter the haven

Hold on alongest the shoare Northeast unto the Naze, where two trees stand upon a high hill: when they are both in one cond North Northwest, by the markes of Harwich until you come before the Haven … If you will beare in with Harwich set the broad tower standing westward of Harwich in the wood Southward of Harwich, and enter northwest and by North and north northwest until you are cleare of the fishers stakes. Then turn in westward or northward as you please and anker in 6 or 7 fathom.

Since the 1660s, a coal-fired light was being lit above the town gate (the 'high lighthouse') with six great candles on the town green, paid for by one penny per ton levy for coals and a three-halfpence levy for other goods upon every coaster. Together with the 'low lighthouse,' 150 yards apart, the two beacons did more than alert ships to the approach of land in foggy weather — by navigating between the two lights, mariners knew they were following the right course into the haven. In particular, these lights guided boats away from the 'Andrews' sand-bank, a hazardous bar near the haven entrance south-east from Landguard Fort. As the mid-eighteenth century cartographical publishers, Mount and Page, advised, the Andrews

"is a narrow point of small stones that lie out from Landguard Fort half a mile and drieth at low water. The marks to carry you clear is to bring the two lighthouses together."

Additionally there were beacons and other markers. From 1567 these were organised by Trinity House which had been created by royal charter in 1514 "so that they might regulate the pilotage of ships in the King's streams." In 1835, Trinity House also assumed direct responsibility for the lighthouses as well. Previously, they had been in the hands of the Rebow family who recouped their investment and running costs by charging dues on all ships using the haven.

The Andrews was far from being the only hazard to avoid. There was also 'The Altar.' Page and Mount warned that next to this ridge, opposite Landguard Fort

the channel here at low water is not more than a cable's length in breadth. On the Fort side there is five fathom and on the Altar six feet of water. A cable's length within the fort lies a cross ridge on which at low water is but fifteen feet, it lieth quite across the channel. In coming in you must sail along the beach on the Fort side to avoid the Gristle and the flat from the Point called the Guard that lieth off from Harwich town till you bring open Manningtree water and a high tree that stands to the Southward of the Hill point next above Harwich town. Then you may anchor where you please in five, six or seven fathom, taking care of a long spit of sand that runs off Shotley Point cross to Ipswich Water.

FIG 20
*Harwich's Low
Lighthouse, painted
by John Constable
in 1820*

In 1683, the Corporation of Harwich paid Captain Greenvil Collins £10 (he promise to pay back £5 on completion to the poor of the parish) to produce 'a moste excellent work in surveying of all the sea costs and sandes.' This provided the information for the first accurate chart of the haven in 1686. Subsequent surveys demonstrated that the pace of change to the coastline and the harbour entrance was intensifying. The lessons from failing to keep waterways in good repair were clear from what was happening along the Dutch coast. There the Maas, which provided the entrance to Rotterdam, was gradually silting up. The result was the costly construction of new canals in the nineteenth century and, eventually, to the New Waterway in 1871.

Harwich now faced similar threats. During the late eighteenth and early nineteenth century, coastal erosion at Beacon Cliff on the south (Essex) bank to the haven's entrance continued at an alarming rate. The sea whipped away the clay coastline by less than 40 feet between 1709 and 1756. At less than a foot a year, this was hardly calamitous. But in the succeeding half century nearer 80 feet was lost. Then, between 1804 and 1841, erosion took away 350 feet. Vicar's Field was consumed by the sea shortly after 1807. The sea was also beginning to encroach at Lower Dovercourt which, had it gone unchecked, would have been ruinous.

What caused this hastening pace of erosion? The single most obvious culprit was the decision to dredge-up over a million tons of septaria cement stone from 1812 onwards. Doing so was profitable and not just for the contractors: the task employed up to 500 men, doing much to bring money into Harwich to replace the dwindling income from fishing and, after victory over Napoleon in 1815, the rapid decline of the Royal Naval Yard and, soon after, the end of the packet boat service. However, it was short-sighted. The dredging at Cobbold's Point removed a natural breakwater while that at Beacon Hill hastened the cliff's collapse. This widened the estuary and in doing so weakened the scrubbing power of the flood and ebb steams on the estuary floor. Rather than being swept away, shingle built up. Left unchecked, the haven appeared doomed as a major port.

By the beginning of the 1840s, the perilous situation was recognised and Harwich's town corporation commissioned a Royal Navy hydrographer, Captain John Washington of the steamer, HMS *Shearwater*, to survey the haven. On 19 January 1843 he sent his report to the Secretary of the Admiralty. It made for sobering reading:

> The port of Harwich, owing to its general depth of water, its extent, the shelter it affords, and immediate communication with the sea, is one of the most valuable on our eastern shores; and although the rivers Thames and Humber afford shelter by running far up them, yet Harwich, from its easy access by night or by day, in all weathers, and in all states of the tide, is the only harbour of refuge, properly so called, on the East coast of England.
>
> … in easterly gales [it] has given shelter to 500 sail of shipping at once, great changes have

taken place within the last 20 years, owing to the falling down and washing away of Beacon Cliff on the western side of the entrance, and the growing out of Landguard Point on the eastern side, whereby the harbour is already much deteriorated, and is daily becoming worse.

To the truth of this statement I can bear the fullest testimony from my own observations during the last two years, and all the evidence I can obtain, goes to show that the sole and immediate cause of the damage in question is, the digging up and carrying away the cement stone from the foot of Beacon Cliff, and Felixstow Ledge.

… But while the sea has gained upon the land on the western side of the harbour, the contrary has taken place on the eastern or Suffolk side, where within the last 30 years Landguard Point has grown out 1,500 feet, thereby blocking up the chief entrance into the harbour; so that where in the year 1804 was a channel seven fathoms deep at low water, is now a shingle beach as many feet above high-water mark.… the two lighthouses, erected but a few years since at great expense, are no longer a safe leading mark into the harbour; on the contrary, they have already caused serious damage to several vessels by running them ashore.

These are great and increasing evils, and demand immediate attention, if the port of Harwich is to be preserved.

To remedy the situation, Washington proposed "an immediate stop" to any further cement

FIG 21
Captain John Washington

stone exaction and "to replace by an inexpensive breakwater of rough stone run out about 800 yards, the natural barrier which has been carried away from the foot of Beacon Cliff, whereby the ebb stream will be again directed against Landguard Point, so as to prevent its extension, and the shelter to the outer part of the harbour in northernly and southernly gales will be restored." He also favoured the creation of a pile jetty along the northern face of the town and the dredging of channels to a depth of 15 feet at low water (27 feet at high water) and the placing of a new red harbour light to replace what erosion had made the misleading directions offered by the existing two lighthouses.

Washington concluded by pointing out that preserving Harwich's effectiveness as a port was not only important because of the quality of the haven it offered to British ships from the storms of nature and of war, but because the imminent extension of the railway line to Harwich would likely make it once more a major centre for the Post Office's continental mail service, supplemented by the building of new steamers to reinvigorate its passenger routes to Europe. "Under these points of view," concluded Washington, "but chiefly as the Packet Station for all northern and central Europe, the preservation of this port appears to be of national importance."

Captain Washington was duly appointed to a ten-man commission established by a House of Commons Select Committee to examine the options for constructing a Harbour of Refuge in the English Channel. His input was evident in the commission's report in August 1844 which recommended two harbours of refuge at opposite approaches to the Channel — one at Portland and the other at Harwich, the latter being both

> remarkably well situated for the convenience of the North Sea squadron … and for the protection of the mouth of the Thames. It is the only safe harbour along this coast and is in the direct line of traffic between the Thames and

the Northern ports of the kingdom. As well as of the trade from the North of Europe.

A breakwater at Beacon Cliff and the dredging of the harbour were recommended as minimum necessities. In 1845, the Royal Commission on Tidal Harbours accepted the need for action. The following year, the Admiralty began the work of rescuing Harwich from its own folly.

The work took ten years, cost £130,000 (£58,000 on the breakwater; £72,000 on dredging) and followed the spirit, if not the letter, of what Washington had proposed. A breakwater was created jutting out of Beacon Cliff by the laying of a stone groyne. During construction, the original proposed length of 800 yards was reduced to 520 yards. Dredging excavated 815,000 cubic yards of the estuary's bed.

The sum effect of this work was to retard the rate of the haven's decline, rather than to put a halt to it. More needed to be done.

Supported by the town corporations of Harwich and Ipswich, in 1861 Captain Washington — who had since 1855 been Hydrographer of the Royal Navy — sent a fresh memorandum appealing to the Government to construct a breakwater at Landguard. The cost would be at least £10,000. But who should pay for it? Harwich's anchorage dues, which had averaged around £18 per annum over the previous five years, were clearly insufficient to cover the cost of construction and the borough council was already labouring under the loan repayment costs from improvements to the quay and pier in 1851. Nor was Ipswich in a position to help shoulder the bill, since it was struggling to pay the interest on a £108,000 loan it had taken out on its stretch of the Orwell and the building of a floating basin. Believing that it had already undertaken great expense on Harwich's behalf over the previous decade, the Admiralty was reluctant to divert more of its resources in that direction.

In May 1862 a new House of Commons select committee was established to consider how Harwich's prospects as a harbour of refuge might be improved. The ten man committee was chaired by Captain Henry Jervis-White-Jervis (who, helpfully, was the sitting Conservative MP for Harwich) and included Sir Stafford Northcote, a rising figure in the Conservative Party who was later Disraeli's Chancellor of the Exchequer. Although the committee only deliberated for a month, the evidence it heard was overwhelming, not least from Washington. He observed that a 42 ft deep (at low water) channel through which he had sailed into the Harwich haven in 1826 was now a beach that was six feet above the high water line. Without further work, the haven would soon be unusable for big ships.

This intervention was the last major contribution Washington made to securing a future for Harwich. Promoted that same year to the rank of Vice-Admiral, he was greatly distressed by the way in which losses at sea were constantly being blamed — however unfairly — upon the work of his hydrographer's office. When the Navy refused his entreaties not to send his son back out on another long foreign posting immediately after his lengthy tour of service in the South China Sea, his health gave way. Aged 63, he was already worn out and sought to recuperate in Switzerland. He died at Le Havre on his way back home, on 16 September 1863. The cause of death was put as "nervous ailments."

Yet, for Harwich, his work was done and his arguments were backed up by the other witnesses brought before the MPs. Scarcely had the Select Committee finished hearing from the last of them than it issued its report. Its recommendations went far beyond endorsing the need for a breakwater off Landguard Point. What the Committee suggested formed the basis for the Harwich Harbour Act of 1863 and, with it, the creation of a conservancy body — what is now the Harwich Haven Authority.

The Harwich Harbour Act, 1863

On 2 June 1862, shortly before MPs departed Westminster for Parliament's summer recess, the House of Commons select committee on 'harbours of refuge' issued its report. It lamented how jurisdiction over the haven was over-lapping and confused

> The borough of Harwich having no jurisdiction beyond its foreshore, Ipswich Dock Commission having control of the greater part of the Orwell, Ipswich Corporation jurisdiction over the harbour of Harwich from Shotley Gate to Landguard Point and there appearing to be authority over the Stour.
>
> There appears to be no likelihood of these interests combining for the general welfare.
>
> It is of importance that the harbour and entrance to the estuary should be placed under one general authority … a Bill should be brought in by the Board of Trade authorising the placing of the Stour, Harwich harbour and such portions of the Orwell as are not under the Dock Commissioners of Ipswich, under the supervision of a Conservancy Board representing the local interests of Harwich, Mistley and Ipswich, in addition to certain members to be named by the Board of Trade … That this Conservancy Board shall have power to levy such dues … as may be necessary to defray the cost of improvement and maintenance … and all dues raised on shipping [should be applied] to shipping purposes … That, as national interests are concerned, some assistance should be given by the Government.

Less than 14 months later these principles were enshrined in law with the passage of the Harwich Harbour Act on 28 July 1863.

The Act abolished the various Harwich and Ipswich-based levy-raising bodies that claimed rights over the haven, replacing them with one authority, the Harwich Harbour Conservancy Board (what is now the Harwich Haven Authority). Henceforth, it alone would have the right to levy the haven's users for the maintenance and improvement of the estuary and its facilities. The Schedule annexed to the Act stipulated that it could do so at a rate of one penny per ton on all vessels of, or exceeding, 30 tons. Those under 30 tons were to come and go for free. Additionally, the Conservancy Board was to enforce by-laws aimed at improving navigation in the estuary.

In particular, the Board was tasked with addressing the hazardous build-up of shingle beyond Landguard Point and for dredging the haven — on the proviso that all proposals were first to be approved by both the Board of Trade and (given its strategic significance) the Secretary of State for War. Obviously, it would take time for the new entity to accumulate sufficient revenue to undertake the major and most pressing tasks, thus there was an acknowledgement that initially the taxpayer would be called upon for an additional contribution. However, the Conservancy Board would enjoy the right to buy and sell property and to borrow (albeit that the size of the loan would likely be dependent upon the Board showing it was raising sufficient revenue as a security), with its accounts to be audited by the Board of Trade.

The Act stipulated that the Conservancy Board should be run by nine conservators. One would be appointed each by the Treasury, the Admiralty, Trinity House, the corporation of Harwich, the corporation of Ipswich and the Ipswich Dock Commission. Two were to be appointed by the Board of Trade while the ninth member was to be annually elected by all those who owned or lived on land in Mistley and Manningtree. Thus, of the nine members of the Board, four were appointed by the Government.

The bill did not pass through all its parliamentary stages without opposition — less because of the principles it enshrined and institutions it established as because it involved another cost to the public purse. The leading dissident was James Clay, a Liberal MP who besides devoting much of his life to mastering the game of whist also happened to be the parliamentary representative for Harwich's east-coast rival port of Hull. During the debate in the

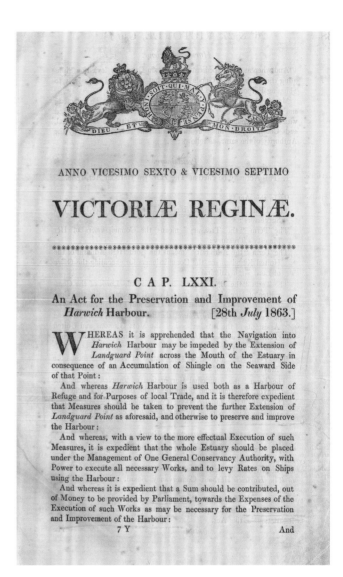

FIG 22
Title page of the Harwich Harbour Act, 1863

Commons on 19 June 1863, Hansard records Clay's protestation that

> the grant of public money proposed to the locality was, in his opinion, entirely without justification. It was as causeless an expenditure of public money as any he knew. If the grant were made to Harwich Harbour, a place not at all recommended in the Report of the Harbour Commission, they might as well set aside the recommendations of that Report altogether. It was far from his intention to denounce the Bill as a railway job, but it looked like an attempt to get the public money for the improvement of a harbour which it was the interest of the Great Eastern Railway to have improved, but not that of the public. He repudiated the taunt that it was because he represented a rival port that he made any opposition to the Bill. Hull did not require to be nursed at the expense of the nation; and if even any such demand were made, he should oppose it.

Clay's efforts to present the bill as a means of diverting public funds towards an investment from which the chief beneficiary would be the Great Eastern Railway (which having extended its railway line to Harwich dock, was poised to operate steamers from there to the continent) were vigorously denied by other MPs. Harwich's member, Henry Jervis-White-Jervis, protested that the measure was necessary because the select committee of which he was chairman had recommended it and not because he was MP for Harwich for whose sake "it did not matter whether the silting up continued or not … [since] the trade of the borough was not dependent upon it." This was perhaps the most disingenuous contribution to the entire debate.

An effort to remove the clause in the bill granting £10,000 of taxpayers' money to prevent the shingle-build up beyond Landguard Point was put to the vote but defeated by 153 votes to 24. Without this sum, it would have been years — perhaps a fatal delay — before the Harwich Harbour Conservancy Board would have been in a position to tackle the greatest threat to the haven.

The Conservancy Board —
The First Fifty Years

At their first meeting, the members of the Harwich Harbour Conservancy Board elected Lord Alfred Paget as their chairman. A younger son of the Earl of Anglesey, Paget had been a soldier and (until his defeat in the 1865 general election) the Liberal MP for Litchfield as well as a former equerry to the Queen. F.B. Philbrick became the clerk (salary £65 per annum) and stayed in that post for five years. C.S. Tovell became Harbour Master and rate-collector on a salary of £100 a year along with a 12.5 per cent commission on all the rates he collected.

Far from the 1863 Act of Parliament settling the Conservancy Board's competences and revenues, almost immediately the Board pushed for changes. The most important dispute concerned the scale of duties laid down. In particular, the Conservancy Board wanted to encourage regular users and proposed that after they had paid for five anchorages in advance, they should enjoy free use for the remainder of the year. Additionally, the Board felt that the rates laid down by Parliament penalised some yacht-owners. Upon this point the

Board was heavily lobbied by the Royal Harwich Yacht Club which had been formed in 1843 and, prior to the Act, had enjoyed various privileges. The sailing regattas that the Club organised were becoming major events in Britain's sporting calendar, bringing trade, income and glamour to the town.

To these petitions the Board of Trade initially appeared unmoved. Nevertheless in April 1864, it agreed with the Conservancy Board a new tariff. This compromise fixed levies at one penny per ton for vessels of 30 tons or more and half a penny per ton for vessels in ballast, yachts and fishing vessels. There would be payment exemptions for steamers after they had paid twenty levies in a year and for those under sail after ten levies in the year. Subsequent legislation extended other powers to the Conservancy Board which had not been thought of at the time the original bill was framed including the right to compulsorily purchase land necessary for vital conservation purposes, a deficiency made good by new legislation in 1865.

Thus it was that the first two years were largely consumed with establishing the Board's rights and the means through which it could enact its responsibilities, not least its ability to access grants and loans. Gaining (limited) compulsory purchase rights in 1865 speeded-up an otherwise protracted campaign to construct the urgently needed breakwater at Landguard Point. In its first years, the Board was taking-in an average of £1,240 a year in levies which would not have been enough to carry out its work but for a Treasury grant and a loan.

FIG 24 & 25
The gentle curve of Peter Bruff's groyne and jetty at Landguard Point

It was with the Treasury's assistance that the construction of the critical breakwater was undertaken. Overseen by the engineer, Peter Bruff, it took the form of a timber groyne, with a hearting of concrete and stone rubble, which extended 1,350 feet south-east from the Landguard coast. Successive surveys thereafter began to report its success, with the slow but continual recession of the shingle-bank and the improvement to the haven entrance. A great victory, slowly but methodically, was being won against the tide.

Peter Schuyler Bruff (1811–1900) was the Board's engineer from 1863 until his retirement in 1895, when he was succeeded by his assistant, Thomas Miller. In 1849 he had been commissioned by the Eastern Counties Railway to construct the 32 arch, Chappel viaduct, a magnificent feat of brick engineering 75 ft above the Colne Valley. When the railway company refused to back Bruff's scheme to carry the line beyond Colchester to Ipswich, he founded his own company, the Eastern Union Railway, and personally oversaw the line's construction, including the tunnelling through Stoke Hill, the design of the curved tunnel that resulted being the first of its kind. During the 1860s and 1870s he invested a lot of his own money in transforming Walton-on-the-Naze and Clacton-on-Sea into seaside resorts (effectively creating Clacton almost from scratch), building piers, hotels and housing there. He also concerned himself with finding decent water-supplies for Harwich (which after various false-starts he eventually identified, ten miles away at Mistley) and Colchester and in improving Ipswich's drainage system. He relaxed

by being an enthusiastic member (and chairman) of the Royal Harwich Yacht Club.

The role of the Great Eastern Railway in connecting Harwich to the expanding rail network and bringing to the port steamer services to the continent was critical to Harwich's future as an international port. But with the Conservancy Board, the company's relationship was sometimes testy. The Board succeeded in blocking the Railway's plans for a new jetty on the grounds that it would hinder navigation in the haven.

When, in 1872, a bill was brought before Parliament to allow the Great Eastern Railway to construct a quay at Ray Island (what became Parkeston Quay), the Conservancy Board originally opposed it until its own jurisdiction over that part of the haven was affirmed. Throughout the rest of the century, the Railway's developments there, in particular the dredging necessary and the construction of the Stour quays, preoccupied the Board's attention — not in opposition but in seeing that it was done without prejudicing either the haven's delicate environment or the rights of its other users.

It was necessarily a fine balance. Sometimes a solution appeared to have been found, only to produce an unforeseen casualty. While approving the Great Eastern Railway's dredging work on the condition the spoil was dumped harmlessly at Dovercourt shore, the Board then found itself with competing claims from Mr Howard, whose Dovercourt bathing machine business was adversely affected by the mud deposits mounting on the foreshore. The spoil then had to be taken to Bathside instead.

Proposals in 1875 to build a railway line to Felixstowe also engaged the Board's time in ensuring that this did not involve the filling-in of Walton Creek. The Board took the matter as far as opposing the legislation permitting the line. Upon going to arbitration, the Board lost and the Creek was filled-in. This was a rare setback. What was remarkable was the range of the Board's activities, which included overseeing and ensuring revisions in the drainage schemes for Harwich and Felixstowe and, later, the laying of the Post Office's first telephone lines across the Stour.

The Board was certainly prepared to take on local interests, large or small. The privately owned quays at Mistley attracted the Board's ire: one owner being slapped with a £20 fine for keeping his quay in poor repair. In 1876, the Board decided not to permit journalists to cover its meetings, believing it made frank deliberation between themselves impossible if it was going to appear in the local newspaper.

The tonnage entering the haven increased from less than 140,000 tons in 1864 to more than 514,000 tons in 1886. While a sign of success, this brought its own problems. There were wrecks to be dealt with — such as the Spanish vessel *Rosita* in Hamford Water in 1881 and a fishing smack sunk two years later when it was hit by the Great Eastern Railway steamer *Adelaide* on the south side of the harbour. Generally, the Board tried to pursue the owners for the recovery costs and, if that failed, pay for the hazard to be removed itself.

By 1884, the Conservancy Board was overdrawn and appealing to the Board of Trade for a £1,100 grant so that the most urgent repair work to the Landguard groyne and jetty could proceed. They were given £738 and told to cut costs to balance their budget instead. By 1886, the Board's spending had been brought down to meet its annual revenue of £1,365. The following year, the Board of Trade announced a review of the Conservancy Board's operation and whether it could be self-funding.

In its first quarter century, the Conservancy Board had raised £27,724 in revenue, of which £26,480 had come from the dues it levied. The budget, over this period, was almost exactly in balance. Salaries had consumed £9,554 and of the sums expended on conservancy and anti-erosion works, the Board had spent £11,000 of its own money in addition to the £27,000 contributed by the Government. What these statistics demonstrated was that in its first quarter-century the Conservancy Board could not possibly have overseen the major projects if it had been entirely self-funding.

The Government did not dispute this finding, it merely drew a different conclusion — namely that, with state aid, the major works of restoring the haven to its pre-1812 condition had been achieved. As such they were one-off costs. While there would be periodic upkeep and repair expenses, these were within the Conservancy Board's budget to find. Aside from one £2,000 contribution from the Admiralty in 1910, the Board received no more grants from the state until a compensation grant for loss of earnings due to Royal Naval use in the First World War.

The one Admiralty grant that was approved came with the completion, in November 1910, of a seven year project to survey and dredge the entire harbour to a minimum depth of 19 ft at low water. Doing so had become necessary given that, in places, there was only 13 ft of water at low tide, preventing any vessel drawing more than 25 ft from attempting to enter the haven. As the Admiralty acknowledged, the dredging made it possible for the Navy's larger cruisers to pass into the harbour.

Begun in 1903 with the intention of dredging to 20 ft, the task had proved a huge undertaking, and ended up costing over £40,000 which the Conservancy Board met from its reserves, supplemented by £10,000 from the Great Eastern Railway (whose continental ferry service was a major beneficiary of the dredging) and by taking out a loan for the same amount. The work was complicated by the amount of stone the two contractors' encountered. Dealing with it involved sending a diver down who would insert a charge to blow it into fragments. Where the diver could find no easy place to affix his charge he had to burrow a hole under the rock and place the charge in it. Some of the blasted rock was then sold to the construction trade, the rest deposited out at sea. Off Beacon Hill, the diver noticed that the rock into which he was inserting his charge was, in fact, the foundations of Henry VIII's battery which erosion had put under the waves. The dredging around it brought up a 24-pound Tudor shot.

By the summer of 1914, the Conservancy Board could take satisfaction from its first half century protecting the haven. Peter Bruff's groyne at Landguard Point had removed the threat of the harbour entrance becoming blocked. Dredging ensured large ships could navigate without risk of grounding. In collaboration with Trinity House, the Board had overseen the electrification of the shore lights. Careful budgeting ensured that, on the eve of the First World War, the Harwich Harbour Conservancy Board was operating with an annual £1,600 surplus.

Harwich for the Continent

The work of the Harwich Harbour Conservancy Board, assisted by Peter Bruff's engineering expertise, saved the haven from silting-up. But without the railway line connecting Harwich to London and beyond, it would have been a port heading inexorably towards a future as little more than a marina for recreational yachts.

The loss of the packet boat service in the 1830s the was severely injurious to the haven's significance as an international port. Its only chance of recovering its former role was predicated upon it being connected by railway to London and for the railway company to operate a connecting steam-powered boat service from Harwich to the continent.

A branch line connecting Harwich to London was mooted as early 1836. Much to local irritation, Harwich lost out in the race to Ipswich and in 1846 Bruff's Eastern Union Railway opened its line from London Shoreditch to Ipswich with a connecting steamer to Rotterdam — in total a 16 and a half hour journey. Eagerly, Harwich awaited its turn to be attached to 'the permanent way' only for hopes to be dashed. After the trains came to Ipswich, a further eight years elapsed before the branch line connected Harwich to the capital, via Manningtree, was opened in 1854, following the plans drawn up by Bruff and his colleague, Joseph Locke.

As the first train puffed into Harwich station on 15 August with the mayor and local dignitaries on board (they had saved themselves the trouble of travelling all the way from London by getting on at Dovercourt), a large crowd was assembled to greet them on the platform. A brass band struck up 'See the conquering hero comes' and the guns of the Harwich Redoubt were fired in salute. These guns fired a second salvo three months later when nearly 4,000 of the Eastern Counties Railway's shareholders arrived in four specially-hired trains for a celebratory dinner. The message could scarcely be clearer: Harwich was grateful for having been brought into the modern age.

This immediately opened up a more positive prospectus. The 1855 annual report of the Eastern Counties Railway Company pointed out "that if steam boats are put upon the route of sufficient power and capacity for carrying cargo and making quick passages, a considerable revenue will be obtained for the Railway, experience having proved that Harwich Harbour can be entered at all states of the tide, and it being the nearest port in this country to Antwerp must, with the aid of powerful steam boats, become a valuable adjunct in promoting the prosperity of the Company."

The prize was worth chasing. With the reopening of the approach to the Scheldt, Antwerp's port was becoming fully functioning again. Rotterdam was even more important: it was the port through which Britain conducted four-fifths of its trade with the German industrialising belt of the Rhine and the Ruhr.

But even with the railway line secured, several attempts to launch steamer services from Harwich quickly faltered, sometimes within months of their launch. Neither the North of Europe Steam Navigation Company, nor the Eastern Counties Railway nor the London, Harwich and Continental Steam Packet Company found they could operate a successful service.

It took until 1863 for victory to come when the Great Eastern Railway (GER) completed its new Continental Pier at Harwich, allowing its trains to go to the waterfront, where passengers would alight for the steamers to take them to Antwerp and Rotterdam (the GER's rail-track went beyond the Harwich Town station that is today's terminus to a station at the north end of George Street with the track continuing to the Halfpenny Pier). For passengers seeking to break their journey by refreshing themselves or staying the night, the Great Eastern Hotel was built opposite the Pier in 1865.

The Great Eastern Railway was created through the merger of several companies including the Eastern Counties Railway and the Eastern Union Railway (and in 1923 the GER became the London and North Eastern Railway — LNER). At Harwich it encountered two local difficulties. The first was the Conservancy Board. Although well aware of the value of the GER's service and keen to reach agreement on dredging practices, the Board

sometimes found itself — in its efforts to balance the needs of the haven's other users — at odds with the Railway's management. A more serious break on the Railway's ambitions was applied by the Harwich Corporation. The real problem was that Harwich's quay simply was not big enough to accommodate the railway company's expansionary plans and the town councillors were not prepared to see their ancient town part-flattened into a goods' yard to secure that end.

By 1874, the Great Eastern Railway was appealing successfully to Parliament for the necessary legislation to develop a new site. The result was that in 1879 it opted to build a new, larger quay to handle its freight traffic, by reclaiming land at Ray Island off the Stour's Essex banks, nearly 1.5 miles to the west (upstream) of Harwich. The new site had two advantages — it provided the necessary space to expand and was outside the Harwich Corporation's jurisdiction.

The construction of the site was nevertheless an ambitious undertaking. At a cost in excess of £500,000 about 600 acres were reclaimed and enclosed by a sea wall, creating a 2.5 mile long embankment. In addition, goods' yards were built, along with train sheds, maintenance works and warehouses, a slaughterhouse for cattle, stables for 96 horses (many of which worked on the quay), rows of housing for workers and a hotel. It was opened in 1883 and named Parkeston Quay, after Charles Parkes, the GER's chairman.

Parkeston's completion initially diverted only freight trade away from the town of Harwich, since the passenger services continued to depart from the

FIG 26
*Halfpenny Pier and the imposing Great
Eastern Hotel which opened in 1865*

Continental Quay. While some jobs inevitably left
the town as a consequence to move to Parkeston
and Dovercourt, that they were being employed a
little more than mile a upstream hardly damaged the
economic vitality of the area. Without the building of
Parkeston it is hard to envisage how Harwich could
have handled further expansion except at the cost
of either destroying its historical and architectural
heritage or prohibiting growth and diverting the
trade to a rival port, also at great cost to itself. Of the
available options, Parkeston made the most sense.

Even before the opening of Parkeston the
service had grown. What had been a weekly service
to Antwerp in 1864 was running every week day
by 1882. On the Dutch side, the opening of the
New Waterway in 1871 allowed for larger and
more numerous ships to reach Rotterdam than
the previously tricky navigation of the Maas had
permitted. In 1893, Hook of Holland became
to Rotterdam what Parkeston was becoming
to Harwich. Freight and passenger services to
the Hook commenced in that year and involved

the ferries making two stops on reaching the Netherlands. The first was to dock at the Hook, from where passengers boarded for the train services that took them to wherever they wanted to go in the Low Countries and beyond. For those who did not get off, Rotterdam was the second stop. However, such was the popularity of The Hook that from 1904 onwards the ferries only went that far.

The design of the ships and the expansion of the service went hand in hand. In the 1850s, the boats departing Harwich for the continent had still been sailing ships (and the haven's fishing boats continued to be sail powered until the beginning of the twentieth century). During the 1860s ferries were steam-powered, allowing for the tonnage of ships docking at Harwich to increase by more than double in the space of a decade. By 1894, the total tonnage had increased from its total of 40 years earlier by over 1,500 per cent and Harwich was the UK's fifth greatest port, by the value of imports and exports it handled.

The 7,000 ton paddle steamers using Parkeston Quay were ten times the size of the packet boats of the eighteenth century. Where sail had regularly taken 48 hours or more to cover the distance to the Netherlands (and assuming these vessels were not stuck in port, awaiting the right wind), the steamers did it in ten hours. Steam-powered technology continued to evolve and the type of craft changed accordingly. The last paddle-steamer for the Harwich-Holland route was the ss *Claud Hamilton*, named after another of the GER's chairmen and built in 1875. In the 1880s, paddle steamers gave way to even larger and more powerful screw-propeller craft.

FIG 27
ss *Claud Hamilton — the last of Harwich's paddle-steamers*

New services and destinations followed: to Esbjerg in Denmark in 1880; Hamburg in 1888; and Gothenburg in 1910. In 1890, a modern version of the packet boat service recommenced when the Royal Mail again began using Harwich to send its mail to the continent.

During the 1890s, the GER launched three new ships for the Harwich-to-Hook service and gave them names to publicise some of the continental train destinations they would serve: *Amsterdam*, *Berlin* and *Vienna*. In the early morning of 21 February 1907, the *Berlin* was approaching the mouth of the New Waterway outside the Hook and was within the right navigation channel when a succession of powerful waves suddenly threw her off course, smacking her into the end of the Waterway's granite breakwater. Listing from this blow, another wave tossed the ship's captain and pilot overboard and, taking a further battering, the ship broke in two, half of it remaining impaled on the breakwater while the other half — in which most of its passengers were sheltering — was sent to the depths below. The rescue efforts were at first hampered by the atrocious conditions. Undaunted, the heroic attempt by the Dutch lifeboat men, accompanied by Prince Henry of the Netherlands and led by Captain Martijn Sperling, to save the remaining passengers was — remarkably — caught on film and succeeded in bringing ashore the few survivors, who had been clinging desperately to the wreck.

Of the 144 that had been on board, 128 had perished. For Harwich this was a devastating loss since almost all of the 48 drowned crew members came either from the town or from Dovercourt and the surrounding villages. Among the bodies recovered was that of the captain, Jack Precious, who had spent more than half his life in the company's service, having made his way up through the ranks. It is noteworthy that the Great Eastern Railway went to great pains not to scapegoat him or seek to pass a shred of blame on to him for the tragedy, stating that

Capt. J Precious, the officer commanding the boat, was a fine man, and most competent officer, aged 45 years. He took no risks whatever. He had been in the service of the G.E.R. Company from a lad, and had been over this route thousands of times. He was the senior captain of the fleet.

It had, in truth, been a freak accident. The *Berlin* was extraordinarily unlucky to have been hit where she was — a few feet further out and she would have survived being tossed by the most powerful waves and missed being dashed against the end of the breakwater while if the storm had whipped up a few moments later she would have been safely becalmed in the New Waterway.

While the tragedy badly hit Harwich's and Dovercourt's community, it did little to hinder the popularity of the ferry service for either passenger or freight traffic. The United Steamship Company brought in a new faster cargo vessel, the *A.P. Berstorff* in August 1913, powered by two six-cylinder engines for the Harwich to Esbjerg route.

Twelve months later this, and all the other commercial services leaving Harwich, were suspended because of the outbreak of the First World War. One of the last ferries allowed out was the SS *St Petersburg*, carrying the German Ambassador, Prince Lichnowsky, and his embassy staff. He had made valiant efforts to dissuade his Kaiser from triggering a war, in the final days of peace telegraphing the German Foreign Office "if war breaks out it will be the greatest catastrophe the world has ever seen." Aware that the turn of events was not his fault, the British accorded him a military guard of honour as he stepped onto the boat that would take him, and his shattered hopes, out to sea. For the first time in a century, the haven was once again a port of war.

FIG 28
Parkeston Railway
Station

Rotterdam

De Harwichboot „Berlin"
vergaan 21 Februari 1907 bij den
Nieuwe Waterweg.

FIG 29
Built in 1894, the
Berlin sank in a storm
on the approach to
Hook of Holland.
128 of her passengers
went down with her

Part Three

The Harwich Force

The outbreak of war with Germany in August 1914 brought the suspension of commercial passenger services from Harwich to Esbjerg, Gothenburg and Hamburg for the duration of the conflict. Few could reasonably have imagined that nearly four and a half years would pass before that 'duration' would come to an end.

Throughout these anxious times the haven was filled with warships: usually between four and nine light cruisers, 30 to 45 destroyers, some flotilla leaders and a submarine force. Temporary moorings and floating docks were levered into place to accommodate them. The Great Eastern Hotel was turned over to a military hospital. Parkeston Quay was requisitioned by the Admiralty and became a submarine base. But while Harwich ceased to be a harbour for normal commercial activities, let alone private recreations, wars are won not just by shot and shell but by the accumulation or absence of resources. As an island, Britain needed to import essentials to keep both the western and home fronts supplied. Harwich's quays were still used as the offloading point for great quantities of merchant shipping, bringing in supplies under official sanctioning. These were still coming in until (and after) the Admiralty declared Harwich a 'closed port' in May 1916.

The Harwich Harbour Conservancy Board was, of course, determined to perform its patriotic duty and facilitate the war effort as best it could. Its clerk, G.D. Hugh-Jones, enlisted, became an army major, and in November 1916 was wounded in France. The war risked bankrupting the Board since it overwhelmingly derived its revenue from dues it levied on vessels using the haven. However, it could not charge the Royal Navy and the Admiralty decreed that nor could it charge merchant shipping delivering cargoes under Government licence. As such, there were few dues being paid. Yet, given the need for continual maintenance, conservation and debt repayments, the Board could not cut its revenue correspondingly. The longer the fighting continued the more a previous current account surplus began to dip deeper and deeper into the red. The Government remained deaf to appeals for help.

While the Board became increasingly anxious about how bad the war was for its own business, the Royal Navy found the haven to be an invaluable resource. It was home to the 'Harwich Force' under the command of Commodore Reginald Tyrwhitt. Acting, wherever possible, in concert with the Dover Patrol, the Harwich Force's main objectives were to be a nimble armada, vigilantly engaged in laying mines and preventing the Germans laying theirs as well as escorting and shielding the larger capital ships of Admiral Beatty's Grand Fleet when manoeuvring in the Channel and southern sector

430.M.
BEAGLES' POSTCARDS.   COMMODORE R. Y. TYRWHITT.   HEATH,
PLYMOUTH.
HIS FLAGSHIP THE 'ARETHUSA' WAS ONE OF THE SQUADRON WHICH SANK FIVE
SHIPS OF THE GERMAN NAVY OFF HELIGOLAND, 28th. AUG. 1914.

FIG 30
*Commodore — later
Admiral — Sir Reginald
Yorke Tyrwhitt*

of the North Sea. Other key functions included acting as convoys to merchant vessels bringing vital supplies to British ports (not least Harwich) and carrying out reconnaissance of enemy movements. In an age before radar, the use of light and fast ships to spot the approach of enemy capital ships and relay their position offered the primary means of ensuring the element of surprise was not with the enemy. In this sense, the Harwich Force was "the eye of the fleet."

Only three weeks into the war, the Harwich Force was engaged in the first major sea battle of the conflict, at Heligoland Bight. The Force came out on top although Tyrwhitt's flagship, *Arethusa*, was severely damaged and out of action for a month as a result. But she was back in action in time for the next major confrontation, the battle of Dogger Bank in January the following year, where she administered the fatal torpedo that sank the crippled *Blücher*. In February 1916 she hit a mine off Felixstowe and sank.

In April 1916 the Harwich Force attempted, unsuccessfully, to engage a German force shelling Lowestoft. Though the Germans got the better of the exchange of fire, the disturbance to their actions created by Tyrwhitt's counter-attack persuaded the Germans to cease their bombardment of the town and return to port. Lowestoft's fate (and that of Yarmouth — which was also attacked) was a reminder to the inhabitants of Harwich that they too were under threat from enemy action. Not that they needed reminding: in 1915, a Zeppelin raid on Harwich injured 24 civilians and, later, the parish church of St Nicholas had a lucky escape

FIG 31
*Commodore Tyrwhitt's
flagship, Arethusa, sinking
after hitting a mine off
Felixstowe*

when a bomb landed nearby but failed to detonate. German bombing also damaged a store-house at Landguard. These Zeppelin raids were relatively ineffective — and, in 1917, resulted in one Zeppelin being shot down. Nor were aerial attacks entirely one sided. British sea planes, taking off from adapted carriers of the Harwich Force, bombed Cuxhaven Harbour on 25 December 1914, an unsolicited Christmas present from one recently ferry-connected port to another.

In addition to this surface fleet, the haven hosted a submarine force under Commodore Roger Keyes, tasked with keeping the seas clear of enemy ships and also with laying mines. In June 1915, one of Harwich's submarines suffered engine failure off the German coast and surfaced close to a German trawler. However, without realising the submarine was crippled, the startled trawler's skipper surrendered. For his pains, he was given the task of towing the submarine all the way to Harwich, whereupon he and his crew of eight were handed over to the authorities. Promoted to the rank of admiral, Keyes went on to organise the audacious — but largely unsuccessful — raid on Zeebrugge in 1918 in which eight Victoria Crosses were won.

As well as Parkeston Quay, the Admiralty requisitioned eight of the Great Eastern Railway's Harwich-based vessels. Among them were the cargo ships, *Clacton* and *Newmarket*, which were turned into a minelayer and sweeper while the passenger ships *Munich* (which, for obvious reasons, was renamed the *St Denis*) and *St Petersburg* (renamed *Archangel*) became hospital ships and survived the war (though *Archangel* did not survive the Second World War). The rest of the GER's Harwich fleet suffered a variety of fates. The Germans captured the *Colchester* in 1916. The following year the *Copenhagen* was torpedoed and sunk in the North Sea as was the *Dresden* (renamed *Louvain*) in the Aegean in 1918.

The *Brussels* endured the most famous — or infamous — experience. The Netherlands was neutral and in the first part of the war a service between it and Harwich continued to run. In May 1915 a U-boat spotted the *Brussels* off the Dutch coast and surfaced in order to torpedo it. Rather than surrender, the *Brussels*'s GER-employed captain, Charles Fryatt, decided to confront his attacker, pushed full-steam ahead and would have rammed the U-boat but for its hasty decision to dive. In recognition of his actions, the Admiralty awarded Fryatt with a gold watch, suitably inscribed. Sadly it was to be his undoing. When in June 1916 the *Brussels* found herself surrounded by German destroyers on its way from Hook to Harwich, Fryatt was taken prisoner. Examining the inscription on his watch, the Germans decided to make an example of him even although he had killed no one and had acted to prevent the U-boat attacking his ship. A month later they led him out before a firing squad. Indifferent to the international condemnation of this act, the Kaiser personally confirmed the sentence of death.

By 1917, the Conservancy Board's financial deficit had grown to the point where it looked as if it would have to default on its ordinary monthly payments. Some claimants, such as Trinity House, made clear they would not seek what was owed them until the Board was back in credit, but others, among them the Public Works Loan Board, were less accommodating. Without either an emergency subsidy, permission to levy dues, or a breakthrough on the western front followed by a speedy end to hostilities, the Conservancy Board was destined to go under.

The Board appealed to the Admiralty, pointing out that it had spent £40,000 of its own (and borrowed) money in the past decade to dredge the haven to the 19 ft depth at low tide that allowed the Navy to make such good use of it. In recognition of this, the Admiralty extended a £1,200 interest-free loan.

Yet, even this proved insufficient and in August 1918 the Admiralty finally conceded that the war was incurring costs upon the Conservancy Board that it could not finance and, accordingly, agreed to refund the difference between its wartime revenue and expenditure. The Board of Trade also, if belatedly, gave its permission to end the dues exemption policy. From October, vessels over 30 tons were charged one and a half pence per ton in dues to the Conservancy Board.

The war ended on the eleventh hour, of the eleventh day, of the eleventh month of 1918. As news of the armistice spread, all the ships in the harbour began sounding their sirens and klaxons. That night rockets and flares were fired off and every searchlight, on-board and off, was switched on, sending arcs of light into the night sky and shimmering upon an unusually becalmed sea.

On 20 November, the site of a British airship overhead alerted those in the haven that the surrendered German submarine fleet was approaching. Harwich had been chosen as the place for it to assemble. For the last part of their journey, they were steered into the haven by Royal Navy sailors while their former German crew lined the deck (they were soon repatriated to Germany on chartered ships). It was an extraordinary sight. Three years after the succession of hostilities, there were still up to 100 u-boats lined up in the Stour, mostly awaiting the scrap yard.

FIG 32 & 33
British officers taking over command of U-Boats from their surrendered German crew at Harwich

Harwich International

The War had interrupted the Conservancy Board's work, creating a backlog of tasks to be attended to with the coming of peace. The greatest outlay in the immediate post-war years was the commissioning of repairs to the Landguard jetty which had not had any work done on it since 1895, despite visible deterioration to its timber superstructure. The work was completed in 1921 at the below budget price of £3,169. A similar sum had to be found four years later for renewed dredging to remove shoals that had built-up in the Stour between Ballast Hill and Mistley Quay.

The other single greatest expense was the raising of the *Marsa*. The *Marsa* was a paddle minesweeper that in November 1917 had been run down by a light cruiser in the haven. An initial attempt by the Admiralty to raise her succeeded only in breaking her in two and after she had been dragged out from the navigation channel in which she had come to rest, divers stripped her of her fittings, leaving the Admiralty to conclude that it was no longer worth its time and money to make another attempt to raise her. At the war's end she was still there and, periodically, causing minor damage to shipping. The Conservancy Board was insistent both that she be raised and that it was the Admiralty's responsibility to pay for it. However, the latter refused and despite repeated appeals, even a question in Parliament, the operation and cost of removing the *Marsa* in 1921 fell upon the Conservancy Board. The experience led it to promote in Parliament legislation which would give it the power to recoup the costs of removing wrecks from their owners. This Harwich Harbour Act received the Royal Assent in May 1928.

There were other positive developments. The increase in the rate of dues to one and a half pence per ton on vessels of 30 tons or over in 1918 quickly increased the Board's revenue and, together with the Admiralty's agreement to make good the short-fall during the war years, what had previously been a perilous financial situation soon moved back into a current account surplus. By 1921, the Board was receiving £3,422 per annum more than it was spending. This improvement in the finances was also down to the speedy recovery in commercial traffic after the disruptions of war and both the Felixstowe Dock Company and the Ipswich Dock Corporation were among those complaining that the Conservancy Board's new rates were exploitative. The Board accepted the criticism and, from the beginning of 1923, the dues were reduced back down to] per ton on vessels of 30 tons or over. This did little to dent finances and despite renewed expenses for further dredging work in 1927, there was a budget surplus that year of £2,872 along with reserves of £14,000. Like so many other sectors, shipping was affected by the onset of the economic depression in 1929. Nevertheless, by 1931 record dues were reported, suggesting no fall off in the port's use. However, the Board was receiving regular petitions to reduce its rates and in 1932 these dues were reduced to half a penny per ton. They were now cheaper than at any time since 1864 (though, of course, the average tonnage liable was vastly greater).

This reduction did curtail the scale of the Board's surpluses as did additional expenses. From 1930, income tax began to be applied on the dues while the previous year the Board had bought the old Royal Naval Yard. The relatively modest asking price of £2,000 represented the dilapidated state to which it had fallen and the amount of work that would be needed to put the area to good use, though the opportunity to acquire such a prime site in the haven was rightly seized. The old treadwheel crane, which had been built in 1667 for Charles II's navy, was dismantled and given to the Harwich Corporation who reassembled and preserved it on Harwich Green. However, the Board never managed to make the most of their acquisition which was requisitioned during the Second World War and subsequently passed to other owners.

Regardless of the general economic conditions, for most of the inter-war period Harwich's story as a port was a successful one. Following the end of hostilities, passenger services to the continent quickly picked back up and to meet the demand (and replace those ships lost in the war), the GER (which, from 1923, was subsumed into the LNER)

brought into service three new ships. Each of nearly 3,000 tons, these were the *Antwerp*, the *Bruges* and the *Malines*.

New services were opened between Harwich and Zeebrugge. In 1917, three military ferries had been constructed to carry material from Richborough in Kent to Dunkirk. With peacetime, there were no commercial takers to continue the service from Richborough but the GER recognised that the ferries could be converted and used to supplement its Harwich fleet. After transporting the necessary gantries from Richborough and Southampton, it was with these three somewhat ungainly looking vessels (unimaginatively christened *Train Ferry Nos. 1, 2, and 3*) that in 1924 the Harwich-Zeebrugge 'train ferry' was launched. The Conservancy Board endorsed the scheme on the condition that the company paid the costs of all necessary dredging.

This 'train ferry' was a freight service in which the railway line went right up to the harbour edge. There it was aligned with the moored train ferry which also had train lines running along its deck. A locomotive could thus shunt its wagons directly onto the ferry and, upon the ferry completing its crossing, the wagons were just as easily shunted straight onto the continental railway line at the other end, saving considerable loading and unloading time in the process. This freight service to Zeebrugge was supplemented by a summer season passenger service aboard the *Archangel* and *St Denis*.

FIG 34
Harwich's Train Ferry Terminal permitted wagons to be shunted straight on and off the ferry

FIG 35
Heavily laden with railway wagons, the Train Ferry docks at Harwich

In the financial year 1931/32, a total of 2,911,876 registered tons came into the haven, broken-down as follows:

LNER (Harwich to the Hook, Antwerp and Zeebrugge)	1,359,042
United Steamship Company (DFDS) (Harwich-Esbjerg)	445,494
Zeeland Company (SNZ) (Harwich-Flushing)	409,021
Ipswich	381,256
Train Ferries (Harwich-Zeebrugge)	204,210
Felixstowe Dock	76,871
Mistley	35,982

Parkeston Quay, in particular, was becoming crowded and its owner, LNER, sought the Conservancy Board's approval for it to be extended. This was granted and in 1934 a larger quay was opened there, complete with new electric and hydraulic cranes.

Despite being primarily a railway company, LNER were now running a major fleet from Harwich. The *Sheringham* and *Felixstowe* carried cargo to Rotterdam. With the *Antwerp*, *Bruges* and *Malines* taking passengers between Parkeston Quay and Antwerp, LNER brought into service three even larger ships (around 4,220 tons each) the *Amsterdam*, *Prague* and *Vienna* to convey passengers, mail and freight to the Hook and back. During 1939, these services were running at capacity.

FIG 36
Advertisement for LNER's new liners, the Amsterdam, Prague and Vienna. In service from 1929 and 1930, the three ships took cargo and passengers between Harwich and the Hook. All three were requisitioned as troop ships in 1939. Converted to a hospital ship, the Amsterdam was sunk off Juno Beach, Normandy, in August 1944

THREE NEW LUXURY SHIPS
HARWICH-HOOK NIGHTLY SERVICE
The Largest Vessels in regular service between England and the Continent
FULL INFORMATION FROM CONTINENTAL TRAFFIC MANAGER L·N·E·R LIVERPOOL STREET STATION LONDON, E.C.2.
OR HULL, PRINCIPAL L·N·E·R OFFICES, STATIONS AND AGENCIES.

THE NIGHT PARADE

HARWICH FOR THE CONTINENT
DAY AND NIGHT SERVICES
THE HOOK–FLUSHING–ANTWERP–ZEEBRUGGE–ESBJERG

FIG 37 & 38

*In the 1930s, LNER turned to the marine artist and ship
engineer, Frank Henry Mason, who in his youth had been
educated on the naval training ship HMS Conway (a 90 gun
fully-rigged sailing ship dating from 1839), to produce these
iconic advertisements for their 'Harwich for the Continent'
services. The slogan spurred the popular joke 'Harwich
for the Continent — Frinton for the Incontinent'*

THE DAILY LINE UP

HARWICH FOR THE CONTINENT

DAY AND NIGHT SERVICES
THE HOOK - FLUSHING - ANTWERP - ZEEBRUGGE - ESBJERG

FULL PARTICULARS FROM CONTINENTAL TRAFFIC MANAGER, L·N·E·R LIVERPOOL STREET STATION, LONDON, E.C.2. OR HULL: 71 REGENT STREET,
OR 59 PICCADILLY, LONDON, W.I; L·N·E·R STATIONS, OFFICES OR TOURIST AGENCIES.

PUBLISHED BY THE LONDON & NORTH EASTERN RAILWAY   PRINTED IN GREAT BRITAIN   1930   PRINTED BY JORDISON & CO LTD, LONDON & MIDDLESBROUGH

In the last months of peace, not all the passengers alighting at Parkeston Quay were travelling for business or pleasure. Following the *Kristallnacht* attacks on Jews and their property in November 1938, urgent measures were put in place to rescue German Jewish children by granting them (though not their parents) temporary visas to escape to Britain. This was the *kindertransport*. The first 200 children (from a Berlin orphanage that had been burned down by Nazi mobs) docked at Harwich on 2 December. Those with sponsors promising to look after them were put on trains to meet their new guardians, those without were housed in Dovercourt until sponsors could be found. The last *kindertransport* to make it to Harwich from Germany departed on 1 September 1939, the day Poland was invaded. The Dutch authorities were still evacuating Jewish children when their country was attacked and occupied, the final *kindertransport* making it out on 14 May 1940. In all, around 10,000 mostly Jewish children were rescued from likely death (few saw their parents again). For those who made it, Harwich was indeed a haven.

Besides the *kindertransport*, in the summer of 1939 as the prospect of war loomed more likely, the passenger services to Harwich were increasingly being filled not with the usual holiday-makers but with ex-pats, judiciously deciding to return home. War was declared on 3 September. The following day Parkeston Quay was requisitioned and renamed HMS Badger. The initial deployment of minesweepers was augmented by the arrival of destroyers, submarines and torpedo boats too, making Harwich, once again, a primary base for the Navy's non-capital ships. In excess of 300 ships assembled in the haven in preparation for D-Day.

FIG 39
Escaping Nazi persecution, Jewish refugees arrive at Harwich on the kindertransport, December 1938

In the first months of the 'phoney war', all but two of the LNER passenger liners based at Harwich were requisitioned for military service, while the three train ferries were particularly usefully engaged transporting heavy vehicles, armoured carriages and ambulances to the British Expeditionary Force in France. Having previously worked the Harwich-Hook route, the *Vienna*, *Prague* and *Amsterdam* were converted into troop ships: the *Prague* rescuing British and French troops in the Dunkirk evacuation and the *Vienna* and *Amsterdam*, joined by the *Archangel* (formerly *St Petersburg*), assisting with the evacuations from Cherbourg, Brest and St Valery-en-Caux in 1940. At Brest, the *Bruges* was hit by the load from a dive bomber and sunk while the *Amsterdam*, with 1,800 on board, was the last troop carrier to make it out of Le Havre.

In May 1941, the Luftwaffe spotted *Archangel* carrying troops off the Scottish coast, bombed and sank her. *Amsterdam* landed American troops on Omaha Beach on D-Day. Hastily converted to a hospital ship she hit a couple of mines and sunk while departing Juno Beach with 419 (mostly wounded) on board, with the loss of around a hundred lives. *Prague* acted as a hospital ship off Normandy while the *Vienna* and *Antwerp* assisted with the Sicily landings.

Other Harwich liners also served with honour. As the Germans advanced on Rotterdam in May 1940, the *Malines* rescued trapped British citizens and picked up others who were stranded on the beached *St Denis*, the *Malines*'s Captain, George Mallory, navigating through the unlit canal channel in the darkness beyond the Hook and out to sea while German bombs landed all around. She went on to rescue almost 1,500 troops at Dunkirk. She was torpedoed off Port Said, and beached, though later repaired, only to be broken-up in 1948.

Of the three train ferries, one was sunk off Saint-Valéry en Caux on 13 June 1940 in the abortive effort to rescue the surrounded 51st Highland Division while another went down off Dieppe on 18 March 1945, leaving the original *Train Ferry No. 1* (renamed *Essex Ferry*) to return to its Harwich service in 1946, where — joined by the new additions *Norfolk Ferry* and *Suffolk Ferry* — she continued to transport freight to Zeebrugge until 1957. Four DSCs, one DSM, a BEM, an OBE and three MBEs were awarded to LNER's Harwich-based sailors for their wartime bravery.

Harwich itself had been a target, particularly during 1940 from the Italian Air Force flying sorties from bases in Belgium. These and other raids caused ten fatalities in Harwich. But given that more than 1,750 bombs were dropped on the haven area during the course of the conflict it is remarkable how relatively little damage was sustained, with the vast majority of ordinance falling into the sea or muddy banks. As recently as March 2012, a 4 ft section of a V2 rocket was dredged from the Stour.

After the end of the First World War, Harwich's passenger operations had speedily returned to their former popularity. The cessation of hostilities in 1945 did not see quite the same return to past form. The European continent had been physically ravaged by fighting across a far broader area between 1939 and 1945 than from 1914 to 1918 and the tourist trade was slower to pick up accordingly.

FIG 40
The entrance to Parkeston Quay

Few even among comfortably off Britons regarded continental holiday-making as their first priority in the period of austerity that followed VE Day. While the first service, a weekly ferry to Esbjerg, was restored seven months later, the Antwerp service did not recommence until 1948.

There were two other major developments. The first was a change of owner. In 1948, LNER — along with its three main rival railway companies — was nationalised. Henceforth, Parkeston Quay and its ferry services were owned by the state-run British Railways (British Rail from 1965). Meanwhile, the days of the old continental pier at Harwich as a passenger terminal seemed definitely over, with it turned over to Trinity House who used it to store buoys. The second main development came in the alternative form of the competition. Flying had been a luxury before the war, but during the 1950s and the 1960s it became more affordable particularly for those doing business but also for the belated boom in holiday travel. For these customers, the ferry made sense (and may, indeed, have been the only option) if they were not travelling far beyond the destination port, but for those heading deeper into Europe airports were beginning to offer serious competition to ports.

FIG 41
*Parkeston Quay
— aerial view*

The passenger service to Antwerp was scaled down during the 1950s and then stopped entirely. The Harwich to the Hook route however remained popular, with British Rail's 6,584 ton *Avalon II* able to carry 750 passengers there and back between 1963 and 1974.

In 1967, a new roll on-roll off (ro-ro) quay was opened at Parkeston (similar facilities had opened across the haven at Felixstowe two years previously). This innovation brought the initiative back to ferries, since families going on holiday could take their own car with them, an option not available by air. Ro-ro facilities allowed the DFDS line's *Winston Churchill* to ferry not just passengers but up to 180 cars on its service between Harwich and Esbjerg. Larger ro-ro ferries soon followed, with the *Prins Hamlet* capable of ferrying 300 cars while new services operated by France's SNCF to Dunkirk were also added. However, DFDS's *Prins Hamlet* switched its operations in 1969, sailing instead between Bremerhaven and Harwich's Navyard Wharf — which was once again an active dock under the ownership of the Mann Group, though from the 1980s onwards focussed on freight traffic.

If Parkeston was to develop as a port then the cross-haven competition it faced from Harwich's Navyard Wharf was as nothing compared to Felixstowe which was both pioneering and leading the most important innovation in freight trade — containerisation. Parkeston's efforts to compete with its rival on the Suffolk banks commenced in 1968 with the opening of its own container terminal. Briefly there was traffic between it and Rotterdam though the main route was to Zeebrugge. During its first year, the terminal handled 21,000 containers.

Having been rebranded 'Sealink' in 1970, British Rail's fleet of ferries — and Parkeston Quay with them — were sold in 1984 to Sea Containers, taking them back into the private sector after 36 years in the hands of the state. In 1989, ownership passed to Stena Line which, in turn, sold Parkeston Quay in 1998 to Hutchison Ports UK, owners of Felixstowe. Hutchison renamed its acquisition Harwich International.

The port could now berth three passenger/freight ferries simultaneously and by 2013 regular giant cruise liners called at Harwich en route to their eventual destination. Additionally, regular passenger ferries sailed to Rotterdam, Hook of Holland and Esbjerg just as they had in the last years of Queen Victoria's reign. To these constants, there were also some major advances with Stena Line operating from Harwich two ferries: the *Stena Britannica* and the *Stena Hollandica*, with on each car decks for 230 vehicles, along with 1,376 beds, restaurants, bars, a casino and cinema. The Harwich to the Hook journey time of these 'super-ferries' of 6 hours and 15 minutes cut by more than 40 hours the time it took the 26 berth *Bessborough* with John Wesley and his sea-sick companions aboard to complete the passage in 1786.

With its container terminal and freight cargoes, its ro-ro facilities, ferries and cruise liners, Harwich International remains a mixed use port. In 2000, Hutchison purchased the 100 acre Bathside Bay

FIG 42
Stena Britannica the world's
largest passenger/ro-ro ferry,
leaving Harwich

FIG 43
*Harwich International
Port aerial view 2000*

site — mostly reclaimed land and tidal mud flats on the Stour's banks between the port and the promontory of the old town of Harwich. Under the terms of the Harwich Parkeston Quay Act of 1988 it had legislative permission (subject to planning consent) to develop the site as a deep water container terminal. The Harwich Haven Authority (as the Conservancy Board had become) would oversee the dredging so that the terminal enjoyed a low water depth of 15 metres (over 49 ft) with the port sharing with Felixstowe the existing deep water navigation channel into the haven.

With 1,400 metres of quayside and a capacity to handle 1.7 million (20 ft equivalent unit) containers, the proposals envisage a major expansion for Harwich International to complement Felixstowe.

As Felixstowe had done when expanding its Trinity Terminal in the 1990s, any deleterious effect to the local wildlife by removal of a section of mudflats would be compensated by the creation of new natural habitats. The Harwich Haven Authority was to oversee not only the dredging but also to advise on the best sediment replacement measures. Critically, it acted as a joint applicant with Hutchison for the development. Following a public inquiry, the Government gave its consent in 2006.

As 2008 saw the start of a global recession it was soon clear that previously forecasted growth in container volumes would still occur albeit at a slower pace than forecast in the planning consent. Subsequently an extension to the time limit for

construction was sought and granted giving the
developers until 2021 for commencement. If by that
date the Harwich International Container Terminal
is finally taking shape, it will be the most significant
development on the Essex banks of the haven since
the Great Eastern Railway named its new quay
after Charles H. Parkes.

FIG 44
*The gross tonnage
of modern cruise liners
arriving in the haven is
more than double that of
the great LNER passenger
ships that docked there
in the 1930s*

The Greatest Container Port in the Kingdom

There had been a settlement on the site of Felixstowe, north of Landguard Fort, since Anglo-Saxon times though by the mid-nineteenth century it was still only a small village: 673 inhabitants according to the 1861 census. Close by was the ferry at Walton's Colneis Creek where coal was unloaded. There was also a tavern, the Dooley Inn, which had reputedly been an infamous hangout for eighteenth century smugglers. Yet, despite being at the mouth of the Orwell, Felixstowe had never made the most of its location, being totally overshadowed by the bustle of Harwich on the other side of the haven. The cart track from Felixstowe to Ipswich was of particularly poor quality, indicative of the reality that there was not much at Felixstowe that merited making a journey.

Yet in 1867, Colonel George Tomline, a 6 ft 4 inch tall Old Etonian who was Liberal MP successively for Sudbury, Shrewsbury and Grimsby, saw Felixstowe's possibilities as a location for a new town. Serviced by rail and steam ferry, he believed it could finally benefit from its proximity to the haven. To this end he began buying the surrounding land from the Duke of Hamilton. The first attempts by the Great Eastern Railway to open a line to Felixstowe from Ipswich failed to materialise. Thus in 1875, Tomline formed his own Felixstowe Railway and Pier Company, intending that it should build a single line track that would pass through Ipswich and connect Felixstowe with the GER mainline at Westerfield. Station stops along the way would include one conveniently close to his own stately home at Orwell Park (now an independent preparatory school) but purposefully avoid serving the Ordnance Hotel, which was owned by Tomline's political and railway rival, John Chevalier Cobbold, local brewer and former Conservative MP for Ipswich.

Colonel Tomline's railway ambitions were realised and his line opened in 1877. For the inaugural journey, he travelled with the engine driver on the footplate of his company's first locomotive, *No. 1 Tomline*. Two years later a contract was signed that passed the running of the line to the GER. It took over ownership of the line in 1887 by which time it was called the Felixstowe Dock & Railway Company. Tomline died two years later. Unmarried, his estate passed to his second cousin, Captain Ernest Pretyman, subsequently the Conservative MP for Woodbridge.

Despite the creation of the railway connection, there still needed to be a reason to go to Felixstowe, and that began to be provided from 1882 onwards when a team of navvies, assisted by steam powered equipment, began digging a dock basin by the recently constructed Pier Hotel, a development

FIG 45

The view from what would shortly be Felixstowe dock of the haven looking west towards Harwich and the Stour. When this photograph was taken, in 1881, steam ship technology had made great advances — yet the haven is still full of vessels with sails

that Tomline had secured permission for through an Act of Parliament in 1879. This first basin was 600 ft by 300 ft with stone quays and two wooden piers jutting into the haven. At low tide it enjoyed a depth of 23 ft. Its first visitor was *Cathie*, a steamship with coal to unload, its second, *Prins Christian August*, which brought Norwegian timber. From these modest beginnings, the Port of Felixstowe opened for business.

Felixstowe also became a place for promenaders. In 1891, it received an eagle-emblazoned royal seal of approval when the Kaiserin, Augusta Viktoria, Empress of Germany and five of her children chose it for a month long summer holiday, enjoying the quiet beach and swimming in the sea. From 1899 GER ran a paddle-steamer service between Felixstowe, Ipswich and Harwich. Within six years, passengers could alight from Felixstowe's latest attraction,

a half mile-long pier with a tramline running the length of it. The dock also served as the home of the Orwell Corinthian Yacht Club, which was founded as an amateur rival to the bigger, and grander, Royal Harwich Yacht Club and as a boat breakers' yard.

For all this, Felixstowe's docks only really began to take off in 1907 when the East Anglia Flour Mills were built on the north side of the quay. Grain silos were also erected. Barges landed with grain and coal, before departing laden with malt and flour. Felixstowe was becoming a coaling station for vessels, including Royal Navy ships. When the Navy switched from coal to oil for its destroyers and submarines (and for capital ships after 1911), the Felixstowe Dock Company spent £6,000 building two oil tanks which it then rented to the Admiralty. In time for the outbreak of war, these were reinforced with concrete.

FIG 46
While digging Felixstowe's
dock basin in 1883,
a foreman and navvies
take a break in order to
be recorded for posterity

FIG 47
Barges and the schooner
Guiseppe Gall in
Felixstowe's North Quay
moored alongside the
newly completed East
Anglia Flour Mills, c. 1911

In 1913, the Navy chose Felixstowe as a station for their emerging fleet of seaplanes. Slipways were constructed on the foreshore from which the seaplanes could be pushed and pulled from their hangar into the water. In the run up to and during the First World War, the haven floated various Heath-Robinson-style contraptions from which the seaplanes were launched: the planes were towed out to sea, or balanced precariously on rickety platforms erected on the back of motor-boats or the deck of submarines. Three hangars were constructed. More than just a base for seaplanes, Felixstowe's sheds were turned over to constructing them as well, under the guidance of the noted designer, John Porte. During the war, their main roles were reconnaissance and bombing.

In 1924, Felixstowe became the new headquarters for the Marine and Armament Experimental Establishment (MAEE), which was central to the development of both civil and military seaplanes. In 1932, a new pier was constructed at the end of which loomed the mighty 'Titan,' the tallest crane in the haven, which was used to lift and deposit seaplanes from or into the haven (Titan remained in place, dominating the entrance to the dock, until it was dismantled in 1966). There were major successes to report. During the 1920s, Felixstowe and Calshot off Southampton became the bases for crews and trials for the British entries to the Schneider Trophy — an international race for seaplanes — which Britain's Rolls-Royce powered Supermarine entries dominated between 1927 and 1931, with designs that ultimately led to the development of the Spitfire fighter plane.

Besides the MAEE's work, shipbreaking returned to Felixstowe: dismantling post-war decommissioned vessels and salvaged wrecks kept the yard active until 1928. But as a port for major international trade, Felixstowe made little impression.

All developments that affected the haven had to be approved by the Harwich Harbour Conservancy Board and, for the most part the latter was sympathetic, agreeing, for instance, to the Air Ministry's plans for a seaplane floating dock in 1924. In its dealings with the port's owner, the Felixstowe Dock and Railway Company, as with first GER and this its successor, LNER, the Conservancy Board endeavoured not to become the agent that bore all the costs of making improvements for which commercial companies drew all the benefits, having made none of the investment. This was especially the case as far as Felixstowe was concerned given that the dues from vessels using it contributed far less to the Conservancy Board's funds than did Parkeston Quay on the Harwich side of the haven. In 1927, the Felixstowe Dock and Railway Company complained that the depth in its fairway had risen to 12 ft in low water and asked the Conservancy Board to dredge it. The Board asserted that the build-up of silt was caused by Felixstowe's own south pier and a compromise was reached in which the modest dredging cost was paid for by Felixstowe but with a contribution from the Board.

Activity at the dock and the need to cater for seasonal holidaymakers helped ensure that the town of Felixstowe's population continued to grow and it exceeded 13,000 by the mid-1930s. With the Abdication Crisis about to break, in

FIG 48
*Felixstowe's Titan crane lifts a Supermarine Scapa while
crowds watch the show for Empire Day 1937. Floating on
the haven is another flying boat, the imaginatively-named
Short Knuckleduster*

FIG 49
Felixstowe's New South Quay, the UK's first purpose-built container terminal, under construction in 1967. At this stage, only one Vickers Portainer crane was available to take the strain

1936 Wallis Simpson lived for six weeks in Beach House (now demolished) in order to escape the attention of London society and meet the residency requirements ahead of her divorce hearing in Ipswich. In the event, Felixstowe offered rather more anonymity than she cared for. As she later reminisced

The only sounds were the melancholy boom of the sea breaking on the deserted beach and the rustling of the wind around the shuttered cottages. No hint of distant concern penetrated Felixstowe. When I walked down to town for the mail and the newspapers not a head turned … on fair days, we used to walk alone on the beach and for all the attention ever paid to us, we could have been in Tasmania.

The place was good enough for the last Empress of the Germans, but not for the would-be, but never quite, Queen of England.

During the Second World War, Felixstowe played host to HMS Beehive, the Royal Navy's base for its small armada of torpedo boats, gun boats and launches. The town's half mile-long pier was part-demolished in order to prevent it potentially being captured and used by the Germans. The latter did eventually arrive, but not until 1945 as the surrendered E-boat officers and crew.

The war's end left Felixstowe in a dishevelled state, a minor port with makeshift warehousing and whose facilities were in need of repair, struggling in a period of rationing and austerity. The Navy left. The Air Ministry's interest in seaplane technology declined, leading to the winding down and eventual closure of the MAEE. Ironically, it was the relative inconsequentiality of Felixstowe at this vital moment that bequeathed it its great advantage over far larger ports.

In 1947, Clement Attlee's Government introduced the National Dock Labour Scheme. Its aim was a laudable one though, as it transpired, fraught with unfortunate consequences. Dependent upon the vagaries of trade, which might involve massive unloading of goods at certain times and a dearth of activity at others, ports had long been places of casual labour offering little job security to those trying to make a living from them. The 1947 legislation gave dock workers security by effectively guaranteeing them jobs regardless of whether there was work for them to do. Half the seats on the scheme's governing body, the National Dock Labour Board, were assigned to representatives of the Transport and General Workers Union (TGWU). This allowed them to block any management proposal for creating greater efficiency and competitiveness if these improvements involved completing the tasks with fewer workers.

Under the terms of the scheme, nobody could be employed to work in a dock if they were not a card-carrying member of the TGWU and endorsed for the job by the union's shop stewards. In addition to determining who was employed, the union also enjoyed veto powers over who was dismissed since it had a veto on disciplinary matters. Sackings were, consequently, rare events. Job losses were not even necessitated by a dock's closure since other docks in the scheme were legally obliged to take on the displaced employees who rejected their redundancy pay outs. Working in the docks was not a licence to print money, but it was, for all intents and purposes, a job for life. 63 of the UK's major ports — including Tilbury, Liverpool, Southampton, Cardiff, Hull, the Clyde and the Forth — were legally obliged to conform to the Dock Labour Scheme's dictates. By the good fortune of her unpromising plight in 1947, Felixstowe was not one of them.

In 1951, this advantage was recognised by Gordon Parker, an East Anglian grain merchant. Concluding that the constraints, low productivity and restrictive practices prevalent at the Dock Labour Scheme ports made it difficult for his business to expand its trade with the continent, he bought the Felixstowe Dock and Railway Company for £24,000.

It was a brave purchase. Now owned by the state, the railway line connecting it to the rest of the rail network was under threat of closure, in which eventually Felixstowe would be left without the primary means by which freight was transported on land. As a result of the neglect and ill-constructed mooring erected during the war, the dock basin had silted-up in places to as little as six ft, making it impossible for larger vessels to use it.

Scarcely had Parker and a small but dedicated workforce begun addressing these problems then the great storms and high tides of January 1953 engulfed Felixstowe, drowning 40 inhabitants and inflicting extensive damage to the docks. Once the tides receded, the work to turn the dock into a major port began in earnest. New grain silos were erected and the Royal Navy's fuelling tanks were converted into linseed, groundnut and palm oil containers. Dredging took the depth to a minimum 22 ft at low water. In 1959, the East Quay was constructed to supplement the original dock basin.

The hard work and positive contribution made by the dock's employees made the expansion possible and was in marked contrast to the low productivity bedevilling Dock Labour Scheme ports. The employees — who were all TGWU members — as well as management successfully fended off efforts to bring the dock into the Scheme when the Government appointed an inquiry into the matter in 1960. New practices and technologies were embraced, including fork lift trucks and pallets, where elsewhere they were feared for being labour-saving devices or introduced piecemeal. One important new customer was the Danish brewer Carlsberg which switched to Felixstowe having become tired of the amount of beer that went missing in the Port of London without any effort by the union or port authorities to investigate its fate. Complementing the hard work and adaptability of the employees was the motivation and vision provided by the management which was strengthened by the arrival of Ian Trelawny in 1955. Trelawny, who had served with the Royal Navy at Felixstowe during the war, identified an opportunity to make the dock useful to the plastics industry by constructing new tanks to store liquid chemicals. A 1,100 ft oil jetty was put in place in 1964.

It was the creation and development in the early and mid-1960s of modern containers and of roll on roll off (ro-ro) ferries that made the modern container port possible. Immediately grasping the significance of these developments, Felixstowe became the first port in Britain to handle them. Its own ro-ro berth, which was particularly useful for loading British Leyland cars — opened in 1965 and three years later, following 13 acres of land reclamation, its Landguard Container Terminal was finished, complete with the latest lifting devices: Paceco Vickers Portainer cranes. Felixstowe was gaining a reputation and succeeding Umea in Sweden as Europe's most efficient port.

Transport links improved too. In 1973, the Southern Freightliner Terminal opened. Besides a direct train link, the traffic bottle-neck for lorries having to pass through Felixstowe was solved with the completion of a by-pass the following year. The spanning of the Orwell by an impressive new bridge opened in 1982 meant that there was no longer any necessity to go either through or the long way around Ipswich for lorries taking the A14 en route for the Midlands along the M6, London on the M11 or A12, or the north on the M1.

Despite these signs of a brighter future, the port's further expansion would be expensive, requiring capital investment on a scale that its owners neither had nor felt they could secure given Britain's mid-1970s financial and economic woes. With £5 million urgently required for the purchase of new cranes, the decision to sell the port was made. In 1976, it had a lucky escape when it was nearly taken over by the state-owned British Transport Docks Board for £5.5 million. Tom Bradley, the Labour MP moving

the necessary legislation, assured the House of Commons that as "a national asset" Felixstowe was "far too important to remain in private hands" and that acquiring it was a step towards achieving the Government's intention of bringing all "commercially-owned ports in Britain into public ownership." However, this attempted nationalisation was thwarted by Conservative peers in the House of Lords who threw the bill out so that a counter-bid from the private sector could be considered. Consequently, the port was bought for £6.8 million by European Ferries Group plc., the parent company of Townsend Thoresen whose ferries ran twice daily services from Felixstowe to Zeebrugge between the mid-1970s and mid-80s.

With its new owners, Felixstowe entered the 1980s as the largest container port in the UK, handling a quarter of a million containers in 1980 alone. Capacity was increased with the opening of the Dooley and Walton Terminals. Scarcely were they completed than plans were made for further expansion with the Trinity Terminal (named after Trinity College Cambridge which, since the 1930s, had owned much of the land upon which the port was now expanding, ownership of the port — Felixstowe Dock and Railway Company — being distinct from ownership of some of the land it was on).

The completion of Trinity Terminal's first phase brought the port to its working capacity. Without legislation permitting it to expand beyond its existing site, it could develop no further. Indeed, the likelihood would have been a future marked

FIG 50
Aerial view looking south-east across the port towards Landguard Point in 1980. Land reclamation in the foreground is underway allowing for the expansion of the Walton and Dooley terminals

by decline, since existing customers would have been reluctant to commit in the long term to a port that could no longer keep pace with their ever grander requirements. As it was, about a fifth of the containers being handled by Rotterdam in the mid-1980s were for the British market but could not be on or off loaded in the UK because British ports lacked the facilities to do so.

To counter this, Felixstowe planned to expand by a further 220 acres along the banks of the Orwell estuary. Eldon Griffiths, the Conservative MP for Bury St Edmunds, introduced his Felixstowe Dock and Railway Bill in the Commons as a private bill in 1985. His proposals had formidable supporters: besides (predictably) the dock owners and Trinity College, endorsement also came from the National Freight Association, the local TGWU shop stewards, and Suffolk County Council.

But there were also opponents. Some were determinedly self-interested, among them those in Ipswich arguing that Felixstowe's growth was to the detriment of their own town's docks (even though Ipswich's were not large enough to handle the containers envisaged for Felixstowe and many of Felixstowe's employees lived in Ipswich). These opponents found in their spokesman Ipswich's MP, Ken Weetch, who rallied 50 compatriots on the left of his party against giving the bill its second reading. Other protestors worried about the effect to wildlife by the loss of a stretch of mudflats and oyster beds on the Orwell estuary — though only 2.5 per cent of the river's 22 miles of banks were directly affected. Recreational yacht owners upstream in the Orwell were concerned about

how the safety and congestion at the river's mouth would affect their navigation. Some worried about how the deepening of the estuary might change the course of the stream. Suffolk Coastal District Council expressed concerns.

All these groups had to be reassured, with some of their objections considered and taken on board. In this task, the role of the Harwich Haven Authority (as the Harwich Harbour Conservancy Board was now called) as a body clearly and disinterestedly committed to the long-term future of a safe and navigable estuary was critical. In proposing solutions and providing reassurance by its active engagement, the Authority was a central player in the process through which Felixstowe was able to grow without unsettling the environmental balance and rights of others in the haven.

Three concessions proved particularly important. The first was that the Harwich Haven Authority, not Felixstowe, would be responsible for determining the navigable right of way as well as other pilotage matters. The second was that vessels from Ipswich should not be delayed or obstructed. The third addressed the threat to the wild fowl, with Felixstowe's owners funding a 200 acre nature reserve at Trimley Marshes, where the creation of a lagoon, shingle islands and reed beds helped retain and attract the birdlife whose habitant on the mudflats was otherwise encroached upon by the docks' expansion. The port also paid for the planting of half a million trees as part of a re-landscaping programme. Doing so limited the likelihood of the port being able to expand further upstream in the future.

FIG 51
Work underway in 1989 to reclaim land
from the estuary for the second phase of
the Trinity Terminal

Even with this work guaranteed or underway, the legislation's passage was a torturous one and it was only after three and a half years of debate in and out of Westminster and jostling from other legislative priorities that it received the Royal Assent in May 1988 — longer than any private Act had taken to reach the statute books in British parliamentary history.

Its passage allowed for the completion of the next phase of the Trinity Terminal in 1991, ensuring that the port could comfortably handle far more than a million containers a year and turnover increased by almost 50 per cent in the next five years. By 1996, when a further extension to Trinity Terminal was completed, Felixstowe was handling double the number of containers that it

FIG 52
*Felixstowe's cranes can
reach over and across
even the most heavily
laden container ships*

FIG 53
*Whether mighty or mini, the Harwich
Haven Authority ensures that yachts
and container ships coexist in safety*

had only nine years previously and employing over 2,300 workers. In that year, the terminal served the M V *Hyundai General* which, with a gross tonnage of 64,000 tons and a deck loadable with 5,500 containers, was the largest vessel to berth in the port. These larger ships necessitated deeper water. In 1985, dredging took the four mile navigation channel to a minimum 11 metres (over 36 ft), while in 1993 a further £19 million was spent dredging it to 12.5 metres (41 ft) over a length of 12 miles

and to 14.5 (over 47 ft) metres in 1998 — this last dredging alone excavating 17 million cubic metres of clay, sand, gravel and rock from the estuary and sea floor at a cost of some £27 million. The dredging was undertaken by the Harwich Haven Authority which, in order to complete the task, gained an additional area of jurisdiction out at sea at the south-east extremity of the navigation channel. No other port in the UK enjoyed such deep approaches.

FIG 54
In service since 2009, the Mediterranean Shipping Company's Beatrice is one of a new generation of mighty container vessels able to use Felixstowe's deep navigation channels

Meanwhile, the sheer scale of the investments necessary to ensure Felixstowe's expansion and the search for the capital to do it brought changes in ownership. The purchase of European Ferries by P&O in 1987 made the latter the new owner of the port. Then, in 1991, the port was sold for £108 million to two Hong Kong-listed companies, the Hutchison Whampoa Group gaining a 75 per cent stake and the remaining 25 per cent going to Orient Overseas Holdings Ltd. Three years later, Hutchison Whampoa bought total control and in 1996 its UK holding company, Hutchison Ports, assumed the running of Felixstowe. Hutchison's purchase of Harwich International in 1998 united the main docks on both the Suffolk and Essex banks of the haven under the same owner for the first time in history.

In 2011, following a joint application by Port of Felixstowe and the Harwich Haven Authority, phase one of the Felixstowe South Terminal development began to take shape on the site of the old Landguard Terminal, with the first of seven, ship-to-shore gantry cranes from ZPMC installed, having been ferried, fully upright, all the way from Shanghai. Among the world's largest, they rose more than 46 metres above the quay and could reach across 24 containers. The port's quays were now expanding by becoming deeper rather than longer with alongside water depths of up to 18 metres now possible.

The South Terminal could now handle the largest container ships in the world. Through such willingness to adapt and expand, Felixstowe retained its status as the UK's busiest container port. More than 4,000 ships docked there every year and by 2013 this port was handling over 3.4 million containers (20 ft equivalent units) every 12 months — 40 per cent of all the UK's container traffic. In this respect, the lead that Felixstowe maintained over national rivals was particularly impressive given that some of the key advantages she had previously enjoyed over them had been swept away in the 1980s by the Thatcher Government's port privatisations and abolition of the National Dock Labour Scheme.

As Europe's sixth largest port, Felixstowe had facilitated one of the most extraordinary global developments of the last 20 years — the growth of China and other south-east Asian emerging markets as exporters of manufactured goods to the consumers of the west. Thanks to the vision of Colonel Tomline, Gordon Parker, Ian Trelawny and others, a large proportion of that trade was arriving on the Suffolk banks of the Stour-Orwell haven. But it was also thanks to the Harwich Haven Authority that the water there was deep enough and safe enough for these great cargoes to make the journey.

FIG 55
Trinity Terminal, with the new South Terminal beyond

The Haven's Gatekeeper

"If we want things to stay as they are," wrote the Italian novelist Giuseppe di Lampedusa, "things will have to change." It is a dictum that could stand for the 150 year work of the Harwich Haven Authority.

It has adapted its techniques, adopted new technologies and vastly expanded the number of other entities with which it interacts, collaborates and periodically contradicts. It has even changed its name from the Harwich Harbour Conservancy Board. By never standing still it has managed to remain in the same place. Put otherwise, it continues to perform the core functions with which it was empowered by an 1863 Act of Parliament back when Lord Palmerston was Prime Minister as a statutory harbour authority with an independent board charged with conserving, protecting and improving the haven within its jurisdiction. That sovereignty is a 150 mile dominion covering the River Stour, the lower part of the River Orwell up to just north of Felixstowe's docks, Harwich Harbour and the seaward area to the east extending 12 nautical miles from the harbour's entrance. Except during two world wars when the short-term necessities of national survival made the requirements of the Royal Navy the paramount consideration, this body has neither wavered from the responsibilities Victorian politicians charged

it with upholding, nor has its right to do so come under serious challenge.

Weighed by the simplest measure, it has been a resounding success. For when it was established in 1863, the immediate concern was not with conserving the haven as it was at that time, but rather restoring it to how it had been in the previous century. Surveys showed the approach to the haven was silting up fast, was already dangerous to navigate for large ships and would soon be impossible for them to enter even at high tide. None of the competing authorities had come-up with, let alone funded, a solution to this impending doom. Yet, within a decade of the haven's new conservators getting to work, the immediate danger had been seen off with, in particular, Peter Bruff's groyne at Landguard Point redirecting the build-up of shingle and unsealing the harbour's mouth. Successive dredging exercises not only kept it open for the elegant steam ships and pleasure cruisers of late Victorian and Edwardian travel but have in the last 30 years of continual toil made the haven navigable for ships that have come all the way from the South China Sea, with a draught as much as three times that of the vessels like the *Vienna*, *Antwerp* and *Roulers* that plied the Harwich for the Continent routes in the 1920s. As this history has shown, the work of dredging has not been a once in a generation chore but a regular activity — indeed it is the single most expensive activity undertaken by the Harwich Haven Authority. Aside from the periodic acts of major dredging, surveying the depths and undertaking maintenance by sucking up soft mud is continual, taking place for a fortnight on average five times a year.

Most of the great infrastructure achievements of twentieth century Britain have been undertaken by, or heavily funded through, the government. Yet, the busy, economically vital, approaches to what has become Britain's largest container port have been kept deep enough and safe enough through the energies of an Authority that makes no charge upon the taxpayer, relying for its funding on the dues paid by the haven's commercial users. By 2000, the dues were levied at 1.5p per ton on vessels up to 5,000 tons, and up to 11p per ton for vessels over 25,000 tons.

It might be imagined that over the last 40 years the amount of traffic in the haven has multiplied commensurately with the volume of cargo being unloaded at its docks. Paradoxically, while the tonnage has continued to rise, the number of ships entering the haven has begun to fall. The reason is simple: the containerisation of freight has meant more can be carried on fewer (but larger) ships. For instance, almost 7,000 vessels (1,754 of them of over 15,750 gross tons) used the haven in the financial year 2011/12, a fall of 2.8 per cent on the previous year and yet the total ship tonnage they brought was 7.4 per cent greater.

Besides this inescapable advance in ship design comes the less easily forecast high and low tides of the trade cycle. In the aftermath of the 2008 economic downturn, both the number of ships and (briefly) even the tonnage they bore decreased. The Harwich Haven Authority's revenue diminished accordingly. Operating revenue fell by £1.4 million to £20 million in the financial year 2010–11, though by the following year there had been a recovery to nearly £23 million allowing for the on-going repayment of loan debt and an after tax surplus on ordinary activities of £2.7 million. Notwithstanding the declining number of vessels and the general economic climate, the Authority remained in remarkably good financial health, always saving and reinvesting its surpluses with the long-term in mind.

Even with their reduction in numbers in recent years, there are still an average of over 40 vessels passing through the 150 square miles of the Authority's jurisdiction every day. On top of which, there are yachts, fishing boats and other smaller craft whose course needs to be kept under constant observation.

The Authority's high-tech version of a railway signal box, Navigation House, provides a commanding view for its Harbour Master and his staff, looking down over the entrance to the haven and to the Navyard Wharf. But neither signal box workers nor air traffic controllers are still expected to prevent collisions by binoculars and the occasional telephone call alone. The maritime version of air traffic control is VTS (Vessel Traffic Service), and this allows the Authority to track the movement of any vessel in and out of the haven. A £1.5 million upgrade to the system was completed in 2011, ensuring Harwich has the most

FIG 56
The Harwich Haven
Authority's Vessel Traffic
Service Operations Centre

FIG 57
*The Harwich Haven
Authority's radar tower
at Landguard Point*

advanced technology. As well as automatically plotting positions, the software allows the Harbour Master to intervene directly and order ships to make different manoeuvres to their original intentions where circumstances require it. Unlike the captain of any single ship or the authorities in the port to which it is travelling, the Harbour Master has to balance competing priorities by all those using the estuary and its approaches and make judgements accordingly.

Critical though the software is, it has not reduced the skills needed for successful provision of pilotage services in assisting the safe navigation of vessels through its waters. In what was the most significant change to its powers since the Conservancy Board's foundation, the 1987 Pilotage Act transferred pilotage duties from Trinity House to the Harwich Haven Authority, a decision that took effect in October the following year. By 2013, despite the reduction in the number of vessels using the haven, 30 authorised pilots were still needed to provide onboard navigational assistance to ship masters. Critical to the provision of pilotage are the Authority's flotilla of fast and manoeuvrable pilot launches — the latest additions being the *St Christopher, St Brendan* and *St Cuthbert* — often having to service the boarding and landing of pilots some 20 nautical miles off the coast, regardless of the weather conditions. Threats to life and limb are attended to by the RNLI and air rescue services while Trinity House — which has one of its main depots in Harwich — continues to advise on the location for navigation signals and buoys. In the event of environment-threatening accidents the

Harwich Haven Authority can deploy its *Haven Hornbill*, a somewhat ungainly but multi-purpose vessel whose range of capabilities include dealing with oil spills and maintenance of the many buoys deployed to mark the 85 kilometres of navigable channels within the Authority's area of jurisdiction. Routine, though vitally important, hydrographic surveying of the harbour and approach channels is undertaken directly by the Authority using its vessel *Egret* — equipped with the latest in multibeam and other technology to capture and process the data on the current status of harbour and channel depths and to determine the need for ongoing dredging.

When the Conservancy Board was established in 1863 its remit in environmental matters essentially meant ensuring that nature was not hindering the easy navigability of the haven. One hundred and fifty years on, the environmental remit is considerably broader and includes ensuring that human activity does not irreparably harm non-human visitors to the haven. The area of the Stour and Orwell is a Special Protected Area (SPA) under the 1979 European Birds Directive and include designated sites of special scientific interest (SSSIs). The Authority has to remain vigilant about the effect manmade changes could have to them.

In particular, the expansion of the haven's container terminal facilities could easily have been to the detriment of the natural environment and the Authority has been a primary force in ensuring this has not resulted — Natural England's survey of the haven's SSSIs in 2010 concluded that they were in a better condition than ten years previously. Such

FIG 58
Wind turbines

FIG 59
The Queen was introduced to Stephen Bracewell, CEO of the Harwich Haven Authority, during her visit to the town in 2004 to mark the 400th anniversary of the granting of its royal charter

evidence suggests that the existing arrangement works well, though further European directives, enshrined in UK legislation in 2009, create a new level of protection — potentially to the detriment of improvements to port facilities — proposing, in 2012, to designate the entire haven a Marine Conservation Zone (MCZ). The Harwich Haven Authority argued against this award, maintaining that such a sweeping designation would reweight the estuary's careful balance between human and non-human considerations too far towards the latter to the potential detriment of the future of the haven and the commercial facilities located within it.

Yet, in so many other respects, the Harwich Haven Authority has seen its environmental and economic concerns to be not in conflict but mutually self-supporting. This is particularly evident in the development of green technology. The growth, with Government backing, of offshore wind farms has been particularly lucrative for the Harwich International Port, which has become the installation port for the 140 turbines of the Greater Gabbard and the 175 turbines of London Array wind farms, the latter the largest in the world and a significant feat of engineering. The Authority has been active in supporting these developments, even providing the Greater Gabbard's contractor with a marine support base while it completes its construction work. With further wind farm development envisaged in the North Sea, Harwich International (and also the Navyard Wharf and Mistley) is clearly well-placed for further wind farm development off the East Anglian and Essex coast and plans are being reworked to make Bathside Bay not only a container terminal but also Britain's leading 'wind port.'

Wind power continues in another form too since, for all the commercial activity that has grown around the development of ro-ro and container terminals, the greatest continuity between the haven of the 21st century and that familiar to Anthony Deane, Thomas Cavendish, or even Alfred the Great and the Dark Age longboat-men is the daily presence of sailing boats. Aside from the yacht clubs based upstream at Ipswich, the haven is host to several clubs, including the Harwich & Dovercourt Sailing Club, Harwich Town Sailing Club, Stour Sailing Club, Shotley and Shotley Point Sailing Clubs, Suffolk Yacht Harbour, the Royal Harwich Yacht Club and the Britannia Sailing School. As if to reinforce the point, looming over them at 140 ft and a landmark on the haven's skyline for over a century is the mast from HMS *Cordelia*, marking where the HMS *Ganges* naval shore-ship had once put cadets through their paces. All told, there are more than 10,000 yacht berths in the Stour and Orwell and the safety of their sailors continues to be a priority for the Authority. To this end, it publishes an annual yachting guide as well as other information and advice both as booklets and online. It also publishes tidal forecasts, a service it has provided since 1933 (until that time the means had not existed to offer long range forecast with sufficient accuracy).

One other constant has been the constitutional make-up of the Authority's board which has undergone only light reform, with just one exception, since 1863. In 2000, following a review of good governance in place at UK ports, and especially at those such as Harwich Haven designated as Trust Ports, long held rights of representation on the Authority's board were withdrawn. Boards were henceforth required to be made up of a balance of appropriate skills, collectively and individually fit for purpose with transparency on the appointment process. Board members were required to have a primary duty of care to the port to which they had been appointed.

Under the current constitution the Government appoints five members of the board as does the Authority, thereby ensuring the Secretary of State's preferment powers do not constitute a majority, and independence is maintained. The Secretary of State

appoints the chairman, which is a non-executive role. The Board largely comprises recognised senior directors from the private sector with a mix of specialist skills to provide the necessary balance. Since 2008 the chairman has been Tim Clarke, the former commercial director and managing director of Anglia Railways and who is also chairman of the Landguard Fort Trust, a body which has been at the forefront of seeing that the fortress that for centuries protected the haven from His and Her Majesty's enemies is preserved for future generations to explore. The chief executive is, of course, an executive role, and appointed by the Authority. Since 2004 this executive leadership has been provided by Stephen Bracewell who has brought with him the expertise and knowledge gained as a former senior manager in the wider maritime sector with extensive experience in shipping, ports, offshore oil and gas development and container logistics businesses. He has held national roles as past Chairman of the British Ports Association and also of Port Skills and Safety. Other current board members include, Roger Morris, formerly of Natural England, Phil Roland, a past chairman of the Central Dredging Association, the keen yachtsman, RNLI inspector and Brother of Trinity House, Captain John Bubb, and the Authority's deputy chairman, George Kieffer, a governor of the RNLI whose career ranges from banking to the aerospace and defence industries. The present board is brought to its quotum with Anthony Coe, previous Chief Constable for Suffolk, John Bradshaw, former Managing Director of P&O Ferrymasters, Baroness Scott of Needham Market, former County Council leader, and finally the Harbourmaster, Captain Neil Glendinning

More than ever before, the Authority finds itself interacting with other 'stakeholders' with strong and sometimes overlapping interests in the haven. In interacting with these bodies, as with government ministers and commercial operators, Stephen Bracewell has become the face of the Harwich Haven Authority, ensuring it has a strong voice in all these deliberations and also by serving as Vice-Chair of the Haven Gateway Partnership which since 2001 has pooled the voice of the five ports in the area and other public and private sector bodies to promote the region's prosperity.

A history of the Harwich Harbour Authority which focussed purely on its committee meetings and board members would miss the grander vista provided by the effect of its decisions, for these are to be seen in the vitality of a haven that risked becoming unusable for all but the lightest craft on the eve of the Authority's creation 150 years ago. This has been a tale not just of dredging, navigation channels and dues levied. These are the means, not the ends, by which the Authority must be judged.

The epitaph on Sir Christopher Wren's tomb in St Paul's Cathedral inviting those seeking his monument to look around is well-worn but worthy of repetition in Harwich's case. For the consequences of the Authority's activities — the survival of the haven, the endurance of Harwich as an international port, the development of Felixstowe from a backwater to the UK's busiest container port in the space of less than 40 years — forms an impressive legacy. It is why Harwich's haven remains central to the nation's maritime life.

FIG 61
The haven looking north-west, with Felixstowe's South Terminal in the foreground

Harwich Haven Authority

Chairman

1863 Lord Alfred Paget MP
1869 Admiral Sir Richard Collinson KCB
1876 Alderman George Mason JP
1878 Thomas Cobbold CB MP
1882 Robert Free
1902 Alderman Sir Edward Packard JP
1930 Alderman Johnson Cann JP
1954 Robert Davis, OBE JP
1963 James Bolton
1975 Lord Walston CVO
1980 Robert Perkins OBE
1988 Sir Colin Walker OBE
1999 Peter Bennett OBE
2008 Tim Clarke

Chief Executive

1988 Victor Sutton MBE
1991 Jeffrey Jenkinson MVO
1997 Nigel Pryke
2003 Stephen Bracewell

Harbour Master

1863 Mr C.S. Tovell
1871 Mr W. Murray
1900 Capt. A. Muter
1924 Commander P. Froud
1951 Lt. Commander A. Waters
1966 Capt. J.D. Gibson
1971 Capt. V.A. Sutton
1985 Capt. I.T. Whale
1988 Capt. R.W. Shaw
1992 Capt. I.T. Whale
2000 Capt. D.I. Shennan
2008 Capt. C. Brand
2012 Capt. N. Glendinning

A Note on Sources

For any historian of Harwich and its Haven Authority, three sources provide the core material upon which to draw. The first is the minute books of the Harwich Harbour Conservancy Board, several bound volumes that are in the care of the Harwich Haven Authority and date from its foundation in 1863 onwards. These records are now supplemented by the Authority's annual *Performance Reports* which are published and provide a full summary not only of its finances and undertakings but also include interesting insights into how it goes about its daily work. The third work — and until now the only published history of the Authority's early years — is B. Carlyon Hughes's *The History of Harwich Harbour.* Published in 1939, it is primarily the history of the Conservancy Board up to that date and draws heavily on its surviving archive, though it also includes chapters on other aspects of the haven's history as well.

Antiquarians and early travellers have not written as fulsomely about Harwich and its haven as might be imagined, but among those that have, the most famous account is provided by the wanderings in the 1720s by the novelist Daniel Defoe in his *A Tour Thro' The Whole Island of Great Britain.* A fuller, though less personal, overview was offered in the remarkable *A Topographical History of England,* edited by Samuel Lewis in 1848 and now available online. Another mid-Victorian perspective is offered in William Henry Lindsey's *A Season at Harwich* (1851) which includes several informative appendices. The Suffolk Records Society is to be congratulated for making possible the publication of *A Frenchman's Year in Suffolk* (1988), François, duc de La Rochefoucauld's travels in the area of 1784. The account of John Wesley's return trip to Harwich aboard the *Bessborough* is told in Sophie von la Roche, *Sophie in England,* translated in 1933 by Clare Williams and in Wesley's journals which are published in *The Works of the Rev. John Wesley,* volume six (1810).

Among more recent histories, Leonard Weaver's *The Harwich Story* (1975) is the biography of the town while its history as a passenger port is summarised in Charles Wilson's short work of 1947, *Harwich and the Continent.* A more up to date survey of its ferry services is provided by John Hendy, Miles Cowsill and Stephen Brown in their pictorial account *Harwich-Hook of Holland* (2011). Readers interested in the details of the Harwich vessels owned by the Great Eastern Railway and its successor, the LNER, will find the vital statistics and an image archive in two websites **www.simplonpc.co.uk** and **www.lner.info**.

For the development of Felixstowe, there is no equal to Neil Wylie, John Smith, Peter White and Phil Hadwen's *A Pictorial History of the Port of Felixstowe 1886–2011* (2011) which contains a treasure trove of images from every period of the port's development with accompanying commentary. The haven's role in the First World War is discussed in A. Temple Patterson's *Tyrwhitt of the Harwich Force* (1973) and E. F. Knight's *The Harwich Naval Forces: Their Part in the Great War* (1919), the latter containing a number of "period piece" digressions by the author on what he presumed to be the Teutonic character.

The *Oxford Dictionary of National Biography* provides biographical details on many of those who have played the most significant part in the haven's history.

Finally, readers will find their interest in local history well-served by the website of the Harwich Society (**www.harwich-society.co.uk**) and also at **www.harwich.net**, **www.harwichmayflower.com** and **www.harwichanddovercourt.co.uk**.

Figure Acknowledgements

Section 1

FIG 1, p. 8
HHA archives

FIG 2, p. 18
Courtesy of National Education Network

FIG 3, p. 19
© National Portrait Gallery, London

FIG 4, p. 21
© The British Library Board

FIG 5, p. 22
© British Museum

FIG 6, p. 26
© National Portrait Gallery, London

FIG 7, p. 27
© National Maritime Museum

FIG 8, p. 27
VisitEssex

FIG 9, p. 28
www.alden.org

FIG 10, p. 33
© National Maritime Museum

FIG 11, p. 34
© National Portrait Gallery, London

FIG 12, p. 35
© National Portrait Gallery, London

FIG 13, p. 36
Daniël Mijtens (c. a 1590 — c. 1647)
[Public domain]

FIG 14, p. 37
© Royal Museums Greenwich (The 'Royal
Prince' and other Vessels at the Four Days
Battle, 1–4 June 1666, Abraham Storck c. 1670)

FIG 15, p. 39
© English Heritage

FIG 16, p. 40
Harwich redoubt — VisitEssex

FIG 17, p. 45
US Naval Historical Centre

FIG 18, p. 47
© The British Library Board

Section 2

FIG 19, p. 50
HHA archives (Carlyon Hughes)

FIG 20, p. 53
© Tate, London 2013

FIG 21, p. 55
HHA archives (Carlyon Hughes)

FIG 22, p. 59
HHA archives

FIG 23, p. 61
Vanity Fair, 3 July 1875 [Public domain],
via Wikimedia Commons

FIG 24, p. 62
Courtesy of Harwich & Dovercourt website

FIG 25, p. 62
© Bob Jones — www.geograph.org.uk

FIG 26, p. 68
HHA archives

FIG 27, p. 69
Courtesy of Harwich & Dovercourt website

FIG 28, p. 71
Courtesy of Harwich & Dovercourt website

FIG 29, p. 71
HHA archives

Section 3

FIG 30, p. 75
HHA archives

FIG 31, p. 76
HHA archives

FIG 32, p. 78
© Imperial War Museum

FIG 33, p. 78
HHA archives

FIG 34 & 35, p. 81
HHA archives

FIG 36, p. 83
© National Railway Museum / Science &
Society Picture Library

FIG 37 & 38, pp. 84 & 85
© National Railway Museum / Science &
Society Picture Library

FIG 39, p. 86
© Popperfoto/Getty Images

FIG 40, p. 88
Courtesy of Harwich & Dovercourt website

FIG 41, p. 89
Courtesy of Harwich & Dovercourt website

FIG 42, p. 91
HHA archives (Maria Fowler)

FIG 43, p. 92
HHA archives

FIG 44, p. 93
HHA archives

FIG 45, p. 95
HHA archives

FIG 46, p. 96
Courtesy of Phil Hadwen et al
A Pictorial History of Felixstowe Dock,
Felixstowe 1998

FIG 47, p. 97
A Pictorial History of Felixstowe Dock,
Felixstowe 1998

FIG 48, p. 99
A Pictorial History of Felixstowe Dock,
Felixstowe 1998

FIG 49, p. 100
A Pictorial History of Felixstowe Dock,
Felixstowe 1998

FIG 50, p. 104
A Pictorial History of Felixstowe Dock,
Felixstowe 1998

FIG 51, p. 106
A Pictorial History of Felixstowe Dock,
Felixstowe 1998

FIG 52, p. 107
HHA archives (Graeme Ewens)

FIG 53, p. 108
HHA archives (Graeme Ewens)

FIG 54, p. 109
HHA archives (Graeme Ewens)

FIG 55, p. 110
HHA archives

FIG 56, p. 114
HHA archives (Graeme Ewens)

FIG 57, p. 115
HHA archives

FIG 58, p. 117
HHA archives

FIG 59, p. 118
HHA archives

FIG 60, p. 120
HHA archives

FIG 61, p. 122
HHA archives